This Book Belongs to the Family of

Our Christian Home and Family

Our Christian Home and Family

An Illustrated Treasury of Inspirational
Quotations, Poems, and Prayers

Edited by Charles and Betty Wallis

Illustrated by Heather Preston

1817

HARPER & ROW, PUBLISHERS, SAN FRANCISCO

Cambridge, Hagerstown, New York, Philadelphia
London, Mexico City, São Paulo, Sydney

When the author of a quotation is unknown, no iden-
tification appears after the quotation.

Earnest effort has been made to locate and secure
permission for the inclusion of all copyrighted material in this book. If any such acknowledgments
have been inadvertently omitted, the compiler and
publishers would appreciate receiving full informa-
tion so that the proper credit may be given in future
editions.

Special acknowledgment is made to the following,
who have granted permission for the reprinting of
copyrighted material from the books and periodicals
listed below:

ASSOCIATION FOR CHILDHOOD EDUCATION INTERNA-
TIONAL: "Sprinkling" by Dorothy Mason Pierce in *Sung
Under the Silver Umbrella*. Copyright 1935 by the Association
for Childhood Education International. Published by Macmillan Publishing Co., Inc.

CONTEMPORARY BOOKS: "The Toy Strewn Home" reprinted from *The Path to Home* by Edgar A. Guest, copyright
1934; an excerpt from "Boy or Girl?" reprinted from *The
Collected Verse of Edgar A. Guest* by Edgar A. Guest, copyright
1934; and "A Garden" and an excerpt from "The Enduring
Hearth" from the writings of Edgar A. Guest, copyright 1934.

DIAL PRESS: "Holding Together" from *Another Country* by
James Baldwin. Copyright © 1962 by Dial Press.

DOUBLEDAY PUBLISHING COMPANY: Excerpt from *Immortal Wife: The Biographical Novel of Jesse Benton Frémont*
by Irving Stone. Copyright 1944 by Doubleday Publishing
Company.

**Acknowledgments continue on p. 231, and are considered a
continuation of this copyright page.**

Library of Congress Cataloging in Publication Data
Main entry under title:

OUR CHRISTIAN HOME AND FAMILY.

Includes index.
1. Quotations, English. 2. Religion—Quotations,
maxims, etc.   I. Wallis, Charles Langworthy.
II. Wallis, Betty.
PN6081.088 1982   082   82-47758
ISBN 0-06-069009-7

82 83 84 85 86 10 9 8 7 6 5 4 3 2 1

Contents

Editors' Note

This volume is a celebration of the enduring Christian values of home and family. We have carefully gathered selections of prose and verse to give fresh hope to all who believe that it is still possible to maintain a family life that reflects the lordship of Christ. It is our hope that the texts chosen will inspire the entire family to see that their life together is a special gift from God. It is in that spirit that this volume is dedicated to all those in whose home "Christ is known and loved and served."

Charles and Betty Wallis

Our Christian Home and Family

What Makes a Home a Home

Where there is charity and wisdom, there is
    neither fear nor ignorance.
Where there is patience and humility, there
    is neither anger nor worry.
Where there is poverty and joy, there is
    neither cupidity nor avarice.
Where there is quiet and meditation, there
    is neither solicitude nor dissipation.
Where there is the fear of the Lord to guard
    the house, the enemy cannot find a way
    to enter.

                    SAINT FRANCIS OF ASSISI

NURSE'S SONG

When the voices of children are heard on
    the green,
  And laughing is heard on the hill,
My heart is at rest within my breast,
  And everything else is still.
"Then come home, my children, the sun is
    gone down,
  And the dews of night arise;
Come, come, leave off play, and let us away,
  Till the morning appears in the skies."

                    WILLIAM BLAKE

A loving wife will do anything for her husband except stop criticizing and trying to
improve him.

                    J. B. PRIESTLEY

You see things; and you say "Why?" But I
dream things that never were; and I say
"Why not?"

                    GEORGE BERNARD SHAW

WHAT EVERY WOMAN KNOWS

Woman knows what man has too long forgotten—that the ultimate economic and
spiritual unit of any civilization is still the
family.

                    CLARE BOOTHE LUCE

ENRICHMENT

Sunshine in the morning, moonlight at
night, the fragrance of gardens, the deep
silence of harvest fields, the musical rattle
of teacups, the laughter of happy children,
the familiar tread of loved and approaching
feet, a beautiful thought, a pleasant dream,
a letter, a kindly greeting, a worthwhile job
to do, a joke, a song, a kindness received are
things which cost us nothing but enrich us
beyond all telling.

                    AN ENGLISH BIRTHDAY BOOK

BODY AND SOUL

A house, no matter what the style, is only a
body while a home has both body and soul.
A home vibrant with love, happiness, and
understanding produces the environs for
building character and strength of all who
dwell within.

                    EDITH K. STANLEY

We live in deeds, not years;
In thoughts, not breaths;
In feelings, not in figures on a dial.
We should count time by heart throbs.
He most lives who thinks most, feels the
    noblest, acts the best.

                    PHILIP JAMES BAILEY

It is in the home that roots go deep, nurtured by understanding and love; by sharing pleasures and responsibilities. It is here that common backgrounds are built, common experiences shared. Wings grow there, too, and one of the surest ways for children to possess them is to discover early, children and parents together, the deep and lasting satisfactions that books and reading give.

RUTH GAGLIARDO

SO LONG AS THERE ARE HOMES

So long as there are homes to which men
    turn
At close of day;
So long as there are homes where children
    are,
Where women stay—
If love and loyalty and faith be found
Across those sills—
A stricken nation can recover from
Its gravest ills.

So long as there are homes where fires burn
And there is bread;
So long as there are homes where lamps are
    lit
And prayers said;
Although people falter through the dark—
And nations grope—
With God himself back of these little
    homes—
We have sure hope.

GRACE NOLL CROWELL

By cultivating the beautiful, we scatter the seeds of heavenly flowers.

JOHN HOWARD

Existence would be intolerable if we were never to dream.

ANATOLE FRANCE

Don't throw away the old bucket until you know whether the new one holds water.

SWEDISH PROVERB

TEN COMMANDMENTS OF HUMAN RELATIONS

I. Speak to people. There is nothing as nice as a cheerful word of greeting.

II. Smile at people. It takes seventy-two muscles to frown—only fourteen to smile.

III. Call people by name. The sweetest music to anyone's ears is the sound of his own name.

IV. Be friendly and helpful. If you would have friends, be friendly.

V. Be cordial. Speak and act as if everything you do is a genuine pleasure.

VI. Be genuinely interested in people. You can like everybody if you try.

VII. Be generous with praise and cautious with criticism.

VIII. Be considerate of the feelings of others. It will be appreciated.

IX. Be thoughtful of the opinions of others. There are three sides to a controversy—yours, the other fellow's, and the right one.

X. Be alert to give service. What counts most in life is what we do for others.

SUNSHINE MAGAZINE

Happy homes are built of blocks of patience.

HAROLD E. KOHN

There is a rhythm in life, a certain beauty which operates by a variation of lights and shadows, happiness alternating with sorrow, content with discontent, distilling in this process of contrast a sense of satisfaction, of richness that can be captured and pinned down only by those who possess the gift of awareness.

LOUIS BROMFIELD

From INSPIRATIONAL THINGS

The joy and enthusiasm of looking forward to each new day with glorious expectations of wonderful things to come;

The vision that sees the world as a splendid place with good fairies, brave knights, and glistening castles reaching towards the sky;

The radiant curiosity that finds adventure in simple things: the mystery of billowy clouds, the miracle of snowflakes, the magic of growing flowers;

The tolerance that forgets differences as quickly as your childish quarrels are spent; that holds no grudges, that hates never, that loves people for what they are;

The genuineness of being oneself; to be done with sham, pretense, and empty show; to be simple, natural, and sincere;

The courage that rises from defeat and tries again, as you with laughing face rebuild the house of blocks that topples to the floor;

The believing heart that trusts others, knows no fear and has faith in a Divine Father who watches over His children from the sky;

The contented, trusting mind that, at the close of day woos the blessing of child-like slumber—

Little child, we would become like you, that we may find again the Kingdom of Heaven within our hearts.

Let your boat of life be light, packed with only what you need—a homely home and simple pleasures, one or two friends, worth the name, someone to love and someone to love you, a cat, a dog, and a pipe or two, enough to eat and enough to wear, and a little more than enough to drink; for thirst is a dangerous thing.

JEROME K. JEROME

Every moment and every event of every man's life on earth plants something in his soul. For just as the wind carries thousands of winged seeds, so each moment brings with it germs of spiritual vitality that come to rest imperceptibly in the minds and wills of men.

THOMAS MERTON

Love and sympathy and confidence, the memories of childhood, the kindness of parents, the bright hopes of youth, the sisters' pride, the brothers' sympathy and help, the mutual confidence, the common hopes and interests and sorrows—these create and sanctify the home.

JOHN LUBBOCK

Great ideas and fine principles do not live from generation to generation just because they are good nor because they have been carefully legislated. Ideals and principles continue from generation to generation only when they are built into the hearts of children as they grow up.

GEORGE S. BENSON

A HOME IN THE COUNTRY

I visited a country home, a modest, quiet house sheltered by great trees and set in a circle of field and meadow, gracious with the promise of harvest. Barns and cribs were filled, and the old smokehouse odorous with treasure; the fragrance of pink and hollyhock mingling with the aroma of garden and orchard, and resonant with the hum of bees and the poultry's busy clucking. Inside the house, thrift, comfort, and that cleanliness that is next to godliness; the restful beds, the open fireplace, the books and papers, and the old clock that had held its steadfast pace amid the frolic of weddings, that had welcomed in steady measure the new-born babes of the family, and kept company with the watchers of the sick-bed, and had ticked the solemn requiem of the dead; and the well-worn Bible that, thumbed by fingers long since stilled, and blurred with tears of eyes long since closed, held the simple annals of the family, and the heart and conscience of the home.

HENRY W. GRADY

The greatest thing in family life is to take a hint when a hint is intended—and not to take a hint when a hint isn't intended.

ROBERT FROST

The light that shines the farthest shines the brightest at home.

BRUCE E. BAXTER

SECRET OF HAPPINESS

A long time ago, the historians of China relate, there lived a family famous for its happiness and its freedom from quarreling. For nine generations no one had left the home, so the household of sons and sons' sons and their families was very large; yet they had no disagreements, no discourtesies, no jealousy or self-seeking.

At length the emperor himself heard the fame of this enviable household, and he marveled. For the sake of other families in the land, he sent an imperial messenger to the home, bade him ask for the elder of the household, and say to him: "His majesty the emperor wishes to know the secret of your family's happiness. He bids you take this scroll, and on it write down the reasons for your household's harmony."

When the old man who was the head of the family saw the messenger, he knelt to receive his emperor's orders, took the scroll, and sat down to write. For a long while he wrote, carefully and slowly, then he rolled up the scroll and courteously handed it back to the royal messenger.

Far away in the palace the emperor eagerly took the scroll, unrolled it, and gazed at its line after line of painstakingly written words. Each word was the same: "Patience."

MONDAY MORNING

Home is a place of heart-keeping more than house-keeping.

HAROLD E. KOHN

The family is an everlasting anchorage, a quiet harbor where a man's ships can be left to swing in the moorings of pride and loyalty.

RICHARD E. BYRD

There are only two lasting bequests we can hope to give our children. One of these is roots; the other, wings.

HODDING CARTER

GOD'S PLAN

Every person in the world is unique. There has never been another person like you, nor will there ever be. This was God's design.

The universe moves with exact precision, but the efficiency of its life is dependent upon not only the mighty and the great but also upon the humblest creatures as well. So no matter how small or great your contribution to life, it is important in God's plan. In Him we all have our significant place to fill.

He loves us whether we are beautiful or just plain. He doesn't measure us by our position, our accumulated wealth, or our public esteem. Our talents, whether many or few, were given to us by God.

The Apostle Paul urges us to know ourselves, accept ourselves, and use the gifts God has so graciously endowed us with.

Remember, you're very special to God, "for he who touches you touches the apple or pupil of His eye."

EDITH BROCK

A HOME

Where two will toil together
   To make their human nest
Withstand life's windy weather
   And be a place of rest . . .

A center of affection
   Where children love and learn
And find in retrospection
   The truths to which they turn . . .

A bond of interweaving
   The all that touches each;
A trust, a true believing
   In everybody's reach . . .

A spell that's cast forever
   Upon the ones who roam,
For time and space can't sever
   The mem'ry of a home.

            MARGARET RORKE

A roof to keep out the rain. Four walls to keep out the wind. Floors to keep out the cold. Yes, but home is more than that. It is the laugh of a baby, the song of a mother, the strength of a father. Warmth of loving hearts, light from happy eyes, kindness, loyalty, comradeship. Home is first school and first church for young ones, where they learn what is right, what is good and what is kind. Where they go for comfort when they are hurt or sick. Where joy is shared and sorrow eased. Where fathers and mothers are respected and loved. Where children are wanted. Where the simplest food is good enough for kings because it is earned. Where money is not so important as loving-kindness. Where even the teakettle sings from happiness.

            ERNESTINE SCHUMAN-HEINK

My home may be made beautiful by wealth of the world, but if it has not love, it is an empty shell.

My home may be the rendezvous of the witty, and the meeting place of the wise, but if it has not love, it is only a noisy home.

My home may distribute its welcome to men of every estate; my home may toil for the betterment of mankind, but if it has not love, its influence will soon vanish.

            ROBERT W. BURNS

I saw tomorrow marching by
   On little children's feet;
Within their forms and faces read
   Her prophecy complete.
I saw tomorrow look at me
   From little children's eyes;
And thought how carefully we'd teach
If we were really wise.

            MYRTLE G. BURGER

Though we travel the world over to find the beautiful, we must have it in us or find it not.

            RALPH WALDO EMERSON

The parent's life is the child's copybook.

Our Family Joys

THE JOY OF CHILDREN

What a joy to have children
On days such as these,
Crisp, apples-for-lunch days,
Gold and amber still in the trees.

Oh to be with little ones
As Mother Nature gives birth;
Buds, shoots, and new-robin days,
Grass and children grow for all they're
    worth.

What a joy to have children
Unlimited insight to be had,
Question, argument and answer days.
To not listen? What a waste, and so sad!

PEGGY URSTAD

Six things are requisite to create a happy
home. Integrity must be the architect and
tidiness the upholsterer. It must be warmed
by affection, lighted up with cheerfulness;
and industry must be the ventilator, renewing the atmosphere and bringing in fresh
salubrity day by day; while over all, as a
protecting canopy and glory, nothing will
suffice except the blessing of God.

JAMES HAMILTON

We never know what ripples of healing we
set in motion by simply smiling on one
another.

HENRY DRUMMOND

Whatever a man's age, he can reduce it
several years by putting a bright-colored
flower in his buttonhole.

MARK TWAIN

There is no greater everyday virtue than
cheerfulness. This quality in men is like
sunshine to the day or gentle renewing
moisture to parched herbs. The light of a
cheerful face diffuses itself and communi-
cates the happy spirit that inspires it.

THOMAS CARLYLE

SPRINKLING

Sometimes in the summer
When the day is hot
Daddy takes the garden hose
And finds a shady spot;
Then he calls me over,
Looks at my bare toes
And says, "Why, you need sprinkling,
You thirsty little rose!"

DOROTHY MASON PIERCE

Happy is the family
    That is bound together by inner ties
Stronger than all marriage laws.

And happy is the family
    Whose members would still prefer one
        another
If all marriage laws were relaxed.

When they are apart they still remember
    The ties that bind their hearts together.
And when they are alone
    They are not utterly lonely,
For the blending of their lives gives
        fellowship.

LELAND FOSTER WOOD

A baby smiled in its mother's face
  The mother caught it, and gave it then
To the baby's father—serious case
  Who carried it out to the other men;
And every one of them went straight away
  Scattering sunshine through the day.

LOUIS DE LOUK

There is no duty we underrate so much as the duty to be happy.

ROBERT LOUIS STEVENSON

The capacity for happiness is the most valuable trait parents should nurture in their children.

CHARLES WERTENBAKER

I don't know what will happen if life goes on growing so much better and brighter each year. How does your cup manage to hold so much? Mine is running over and I keep getting larger cups.

ALICE FREEMAN PALMER

The happiest life, seen in perspective, can hardly be better than a stringing together of odd little moments.

NORMAN DOUGLAS

There is no peace more delightful than one's own fireplace.

CICERO

This family is achieving something! Within this home are gaiety, laughter, cooperation, understanding, neighborliness, community-mindedness and world concern . . . as you enter you are conscious, not of architecture or an interior decorator's art. This home has . . . atmosphere. It is a mingling of hospitality, refinement, and good cheer.

RUTH McAFEE BROWN

THE OLD HOME

It was a shabby farmhouse,
And sometimes the roof would leak—
But there was warmth, security,
All that a child would seek.
Wildwoods belonged to the children,
There was a creek to explore—
Food sometimes scarce, joy abundant,
And we did not ask for more.
We survived all the hardships and
We laughed at the weather.
The important thing, through it all,
The family was all together.

ESTELLE D. BROADRICK

Mother makes every day a birthday of sorts, loading her family with gifts of understanding and forgiveness, appreciation, encouragement, comfort and devotion, all splendidly wrapped in kindly deeds.

HAROLD E. KOHN

Those who bring sunshine to the lives of others cannot keep it from themselves.

Home Is a Place for Care and Comfort

Each home, imperfect though it may be, is our closest approximation to the Kingdom of God. The ultimate human ideal is a Family of Love. We never succeed wholly in what we try to do in our families, but at least we have a chance, which is something we seldom have in connection with larger and more complex human institutions. Within the family we can count on a high degree of true affection and of desire to make the experiment succeed.

ELTON TRUEBLOOD

LOVELIEST OF TREES

Loveliest of trees, the cherry now
Is hung with bloom along the bough,
And stands about the woodland ride
Wearing white for Eastertide.

Now, of my threescore years and ten,
Twenty will not come again,
And take from seventy springs a score,
It only leaves me fifty more.

And since to look at things in bloom
Fifty springs are little room,
About the woodland I will go
To see the cherry hung with snow.

A. E. HOUSMAN

Home is the one place where the world's greatest are ordinary people, where ordinary people receive extraordinary attention and affection, and where every nobody is really somebody.

HAROLD E. KOHN

PRAYER FOR A LITTLE HOUSE

God send us a little home
To come back to when we roam—
Low walls and fluted tiles,
Wide windows, a view for miles;
Red firelight and deep chairs;
Small white bed upstairs;
Great talk in little nooks;
Dim colors, rows of books;
One picture on each wall;
Not many things at all.
God send us a little ground—
Tall trees standing round,
Homely flowers in brown sod,
Overhead thy stars, O God!
God bless when winds blow
Our home and all we know.

FLORENCE BONE

When the door is open no room is small.

GAUIS GLENN ATKINS

FUN IN A GARRET

We're having a lovely time to-day!
We're all of us up in the garret at play!
We have three houses under the eaves—
Not real, you know, but make-believes;
Two we live in, and one is a store,
Where a little old screen makes a truly
    door.
Warren keeps store, and Joe is his clerk,
And Betty and I stay at home and work.
Joe comes around and knocks or rings,
And we order potatoes and steaks and
    things;
And sometimes we go to the store and buy,
Or send the children for ribbons or pie.
It's lots of fun—just try it some day
When it rains too hard to go out and play.

EMMA C. DOWD

From SNOW-BOUND

Shut in from all the world without,
We sat the clean-winged hearth about,
Content to let the north-wind roar
In baffled rage at pane and door.
What matter how the night behaved?
What matter how the north-wind raved?
Blow high, blow low, not all its show
Could quench our hearth-fire's ruddy glow.
And while, with care, our mother laid
The work aside, her steps she stayed
One moment, seeking to express
Her grateful sense of happiness
For food and shelter, warmth and health,
And love's contentment more than wealth,
With simple wishes (not the weak,
Vain prayers which no fulfillment seek,
But such as warm the generous heart,
O'er-prompt to do with Heaven its part)
That none might lack, that bitter night,
For bread and clothing, warmth and light.

JOHN GREENLEAF WHITTIER

Oh, the comfort—the inexpressible comfort
   of feeling safe with a person,
Having neither to weigh thoughts,
Nor measure words—but pouring them
All right out—just as they are—
Chaff and grain together—
Certain that a faithful hand will
Take and sift them—
Keep what is worth keeping—
And with the breath of kindness
Blow the rest away.

DINAH MARIA MULOCK CRAIK

The greatest woman in history is—the American housewife. But too often she has an inferiority complex. . . . Few professional career women live a life one-half as exciting or satisfying as that of the ordinary housewife. Motherhood, the art of raising children, is an endless drama, a ceaseless adventure.

HAL BOYLE

The most important thing a father can do for his children is to love their mother.

THEODORE HESBURGH

EVERYONE'S SERVANT

Each member of the family has to become in a special way the servant of the others and share their burdens. Each one must show concern not only for his or her own life but also for the lives of the other members of the family—their needs, their hopes, and their ideals.

JOHN PAUL II

The light on the faces of the home circle is a more precious gleam than any which shines from star or sun.

FRANCIS J. McCONNELL

Parents are the bank where all the problems and hurts are deposited.

T. DE WITT TALMAGE

Home's not merely four square walls,
  ·Though with pictures hung and gilded;
Home is where affection calls,
  Filled with shrines the heart hath
    builded!
Home!—go watch the faithful dove,
  Sailing 'neath the heaven above us;
Home is where there's one to love!
  Home is where there's one to love us!

Home's not merely roof and room—
  It needs something to endear it;
Home is where the heart can bloom,
  Where there's some kind lip to cheer it!
What is home with none to meet,
  None to welcome, none to greet us?
Home is sweet—and only sweet—
  Where there's one we love to meet us!

                    CHARLES SWAIN

Perhaps the greatest blessing in marriage is
that it lasts so long. The years, like the
varying interests of each year, combine to
buttress and enrich each other. Out of many
shared years, one life. In a series of tempo-
rary relationships, one misses the ripening,
gathering, harvesting joys, the deep, hard-
won truths of marriage.

                    RICHARD C. CABOT

Love is the drive toward the reunion of the
separated.

                    PAUL TILLICH

FLAME'S REFLECTIONS

What is more cheerful than an open wood
fire? Do you hear those little chirps and
twitters coming out of that piece of apple-
wood? Those are the ghosts of the robins
and bluebirds that sang upon the bough
when it was in blossom last spring.

                    THOMAS BAILEY ALDRICH

SPANISH PROVERB

Three helping one another will do as much
as six singly.

Once upon a time I planned to be
An artist of celebrity;
A song I sought to write one day,
And all the world would homage pay;
I longed to write a noted book—
But what I did was learn to cook.
For life with simple tasks is filled,
And I have done, not what I willed.
Yet when I see boys' hungry eyes,
I'm glad I make good apple pies.

                    ELIZABETH H. THOMAS

We ask the leaf, "Are you complete in your-self?" And the leaf answers, "No, my life is in the branches." We ask the branch, and the branch answers, "No, my life is in the root." We ask the root, and it answers, "No, my life is in the trunk and the branches and the leaves. Keep the branches stripped of leaves, and I shall die." So it is with the great tree of being. Nothing is completely and merely individual.

HARRY EMERSON FOSDICK

From BETTER THAN GOLD

Better than gold is a peaceful home
Where all the fireside characters come,
The shrine of love, the heaven of life,
Hallowed by mother, or sister, or wife.
However humble the home may be,
Or tried with sorrow by heaven's decree,
The blessings that never were bought or
    sold,
And center there, are better than gold.

ABRAM J. RYAN

The most influential of all educational fac-tors is the conversation in a child's home.

WILLIAM TEMPLE

All of us tend to put off living. We dream of some magical rose garden over the hori-zon—instead of enjoying the roses that are blooming outside our window today.

DALE CARNEGIE

The first duty of love is to listen.

PAUL TILLICH

Two persons who have chosen each other out of all the species, with the design to be each other's mutual comfort and entertain-ment, have, in that action, bound them-selves to be good-humored, affable, dis-creet, forgiving, patient, and joyful, with respect to each other's frailties and perfec-tions, to the end of their lives.

JOSEPH ADDISON

A house is built of logs and stone,
    Of tiles and posts and piers;
A home is built of loving deeds
    That stand a thousand years.

VICTOR HUGO

The Miracle of Our Love

SONNET 43

How do I love thee? Let me count the ways.
I love thee to the depth and breadth and
    height
My soul can reach, when feeling out of sight
For the ends of Being and ideal Grace.
I love thee to the level of everyday's
Most quiet need, by sun and candlelight.
I love thee freely, as men strive for Right;
I love thee purely, as they turn from Praise.
I love thee with the passion put to use
In my old griefs, and with my childhood's
    faith.
I love thee with a love I seemed to lose
With my lost saints,—I love thee with the
    breath,
Smiles, tears, of all my life!—and, if God
    choose,
I shall but love thee better after death.

ELIZABETH BARRETT BROWNING

MIRACLE OF LOVE

Love is the spark that kindles the fire of
compassion. Compassion is the fire that
flames the candle of service. Service is the
candle that ignites the torch of hope. Hope
is the torch that lights the beacon of faith.
Faith is the beacon that reflects the power
of God. God is the power that creates the
miracle of love.

WILLIAM A. WARD

Love makes one little room an everywhere.

The loneliest place in the world is the
human heart when love is absent.

ROBERT OZMENT

We receive love—from our children as well
as others—not in proportion to our demands or sacrifices or needs but roughly in
proportion to our own capacity to love.

ROLLO MAY

The most wonderful of all things in life is
the discovery of another human being with
whom one's relationship has a glowing
depth, beauty, and joy as the years increase.
This inner progressiveness of love between
two human beings is a most marvelous
thing. It cannot be found by looking for it or
by passionately wishing for it. It is a sort of
divine accident.

SIR HUGH WALPOLE

You can no more measure a home by inches
or weigh it by ounces, than you can set up
the boundaries of a summer breeze or cal-
culate the fragrance of a rose. Home is the
love which is in it.

EDWARD WHITING

Beneath my parents' love for each other
there was something unassailable and im-
movable. On its surface it might willingly
find room for irritation and annoyance—
what love does not?—and yet in between,
where we all really lived, there was respect
and ease and gaiety. Such love within a
family is seldom the subject for words, perhaps because by nature it is silent; but
wherever it exists it may well be the source
for all other pure and passionate affections.

MARY ELLEN CHASE

LOVE

Love is a nod from across the room.
　Love is a knowing wink.
Love is a laugh from the heart's full bloom.
　Love is a pause to think
Selflessly, wholly, of what it shares.
　Threaded by man and wife,
Quietly weaving 'til unawares
　Love is the whole of life.

Love is an arm to support an arm.
　Love wipes away a tear.
Love speaks of love with a special charm.
　Love is a list'ning ear.
Love is the squeeze of a gentle hand,
　Saying what words can't say.
Knowing such love makes one understand
　God in a wiser way.

　　　　　MARGARET RORKE

Every man, woman, and child on this earth
has an overwhelming desire to be loved, to
be wanted, to be appreciated. To the extent
that we can fulfill this desire will we give
happiness and find happiness ourselves.

Love, like a cool, clear water spring, freely
and gladly gives, refreshes and enriches.

　　　　　WILLIAM A. WARD

The light of love shines over all,
Of love that says not mine and thine,
But ours, for ours is mine.

　　　　　HENRY WADSWORTH LONGFELLOW

Love is a simple fire-side thing, whose quiet
smile can warm earth's poorest hovel to a
home.

　　　　　JAMES RUSSELL LOWELL

Let me not to the marriage of true minds
Admit impediments. Love is not love
Which alters when it alteration finds,
Or bends with the remover to remove:
O, no. It is an ever-fixed mark.
That looks on tempests and is never shaken;
It is the star to every wandering bark,
Whose worth's unknown, although his
　　　height be taken
Love's not Time's fool, though rosy lips and
　　　cheeks
Within his bending sickle's compass come;
Love alters not with his brief hours and
　　　weeks,
But bears it out even to the edge of doom.
　If this be error, and upon me prov'd
　I never writ, nor no man ever lov'd.

　　　　　WILLIAM SHAKESPEARE

21

LOVE

I love you, not only for what you are, but for what I am when I am with you. I love you, not only for what you have made of yourself, but for what you are making of me.

I love you for the part of me that you bring out.

I love you for putting your hand into my heaped-up heart and passing over all the foolish, weak things that you can't help dimly seeing there, and for drawing out into the light all the beautiful belongings that no one else had looked quite far enough to find.

I love you because you are helping me to make of the lumber of my life not a tavern but a temple; out of the works of my every day—not a reproach, but a song.

Love is the by-product of our capacity to give what is deepest within ourselves and to receive what is deepest within another person.

LLOYD J. AVERILL

The function of the family is primarily affection.

PAUL DOUGLAS

We are all born for love. It is the principle of existence and its only end.

BENJAMIN DISRAELI

The warm of heart shall never lack a fire
However far he roam.
Although he live forever among strangers
He cannot lack a home.

For strangers are not strangers to his spirit,
And each house seems his own,
And by the fire of his loving-kindness
He cannot sit alone.

ELIZABETH COATSWORTH

One does not fall in love. One grows into love and love grows in him. This begins not in adolescence nor in maturity but in infancy.

KARL MENNINGER

Love is a gift that should be taken kneeling as we take the sacrament saying, "Lord, Lord, I am not worthy."

OSCAR WILDE

I need so much the quiet of your love,
    After the day's loud strife;
I need your calm all other things above,
    After the stress of life.
I crave the haven that in your dear heart
        lies,
    After all toil is done;
I need the starshine of your heavenly eyes,
    After the day's great sun.

CHARLES HANSON TOWNE

To love and to be loved is the greatest happiness of existence.

SYDNEY SMITH

WHAT IS LOVE?

Love is the rejoicing over the existence of the beloved one: it is the desire that he be rather than not be; it is longing for his presence when he is absent; it is happiness in the thought of him; it is profound satisfaction over everything that makes him great and glorious.

Love is gratitude: it is thankfulness for the existence of the beloved; it is the happy acceptance of everything that he gives without the jealous feeling that the self ought to be able to do as much; it is a gratitude that does not seek equality; it is wonder over the other's gift of himself in companionship.

Love is reverence: it keeps its distance even as it draws near; it does not seek to absorb the other in the self or want to be absorbed by it; it rejoices in the otherness of the other; it desires the beloved to be what he is and does not seek to refashion him into a replica of the self or to make him a means to the self's advancement.

Love is loyalty: it is the willingness to let the self be destroyed rather than that the other cease to be; it is the commitment of the self by self-binding will to make the other great; it is loyalty, too, to the other's cause—to his loyalty.

H. RICHARD NIEBUHR

Only those who can love and be loved are emotionally mature.

KARL MENNINGER

A child that is loved has many names.

HUNGARIAN PROVERB

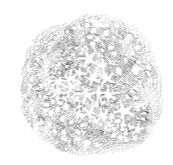

Our Marriage

_____

and

_____

were joined in marriage

on the _____ day of _____

in the year 19 _____

at _____

by _____

Photographs

Two Hearts as One

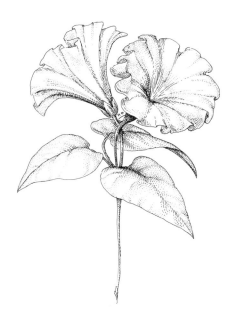

HUSBAND AND WIFE

Their relationship is not like interlocking fingers where closeness creates friction and stalemate but like two hands brought together in a prayerful gesture, pointing toward a love that is greater than the love two people can give to each other. Their love for each other is mediated by divine love. They are witness to love that is greater than both of them and which they are able to communicate to each other.

HENRI J. M. NOUWEN

PRAYER BY A BRIDE AND GROOM

Our gracious Heavenly Father, who givest the supreme gift of love to Thy children, we thank Thee for each other. We thank Thee for all who love us and who have given so much of themselves to make us happy. We thank Thee for the love that has bound our hearts and lives together and made us husband and wife.

As we enter upon the privileges and joys of life's most holy relationship and begin together the great adventure of building a Christian home, we thank Thee for all the hopes that make the future bright. Teach us the fine art of living together unselfishly that, loving and being loved, blessing and being blessed, we may find our love ever filled with a deeper harmony as we learn more perfectly to share it through the years.

Help us to keep the candle of faith and prayer always burning in our home. Be Thou our Guest at every meal, our Guide in every plan, our Guardian in every temptation.

When by Thy mercies we who are now husband and wife shall also become father and mother, may we humbly and worthily guide and care for those whom Thou shalt give to us.

None can know what the future holds. We ask only that we may love, honor and cherish each other always, and so live together in faithfulness and patience that our lives will be filled with joy and the home which we have this day established become a haven of blessing and a place of peace. May Thy blessing and the benediction of Thy love rest upon us now and always.

CHRISTIAN HERALD

MOTHER OF THE GROOM

Not all eyes are on the bride.
Two—very soft and misted ones—
are on the groom.
She smiles
    but calls in silence
    to the boy inside the man
and reaches for him
though her hands are still.

GWENDOLYN BENNETT PAPPAS

EXPERIMENT

Mankind rose to try a new and marvelous experiment—one man and one woman loving each other so much they did not want to love anybody else in the same way at all and so living loyally with each other and rearing their children in an unbroken home. That is the experiment . . . the most difficult, important and promising experiment ever tried in human relationships.

HARRY EMERSON FOSDICK

WHAT LIES BEYOND

It takes three to make love; the lover and the beloved are bound together by an ideal outside both of them. Love of self without love of God is selfishness. Love of neighbor without love of God embraces only those who are pleasing to us, not those who are hateful. One cannot bind two sticks together without something outside the sticks—one cannot bind the nations together except by recognition of a law and a person outside the nations themselves. Neither can two people establish life together without calling on what lies beyond both of them.

FULTON J. SHEEN

I should like to see any kind of man that some good and even pretty woman could not shape a husband out of.

OLIVER WENDELL HOLMES

DAUGHTER

She held her veil aside and reached to him
Whose hair had caught the snowstorm
    years ago,
And pressed her young lips warm against
    his cheek;
Her hands found his; she wanted him to
    know
How glad she was that he was also hers.
The ties she tied were not of blood or water,
But of the spirit, hungry through the years;
For he who raised all sons had now a
    daughter
He could not see, because of manly tears.

RALPH W. SEAGER

Children will outgrow their need of affection and demonstrativeness, but husbands won't.

PAUL POPENOE

A LETTER TO NEWLYWEDS

Marriage is reaching out for the completion and fulfillment in another that no one can find in oneself. It is love carried to the highest degree, just short of your love for God and God's love for you. Married love is a life-long conversation that seems far too short, where each tells the other by words, by glances and by deeds that you continue to care, that you understand or will try to understand, that your loyalty and love will never fail when it is needed.

Married love is the habit of the tender look, the gentle word, the thoughtful deed and the unexpected kindness that go far beyond the demands of duty and far exceed the vows taken today.

Marriage is a revelation, for it is the greatest test of character ever devised. It offers more opportunities for blundering or success, for selfishness or kindly consideration, for fretfulness or patience, for foolishness or wisdom, for severity or tenderness, than any other situation in life.

Marriage is a transformation. It makes one person of two people. It enlarges your spirit, broadening and deepening your soul, making more room in you for sadness and joy, for tears and laughter, for discord and harmony, sacrifice and gain, struggle and success, for self-interest, concern for others and love for God. Marriage is an enlargement of life.

HAROLD E. KOHN

GUIDELINES FOR A HAPPY MARRIAGE

Never let romance wane. The benediction at the wedding doesn't end romance. It only gives you a chance to be permanently romantic.

Never allow both of you to get angry at the same time.

Never talk at one another, either alone or in company.

Never speak loudly to one another unless the house is on fire.

Never find fault unless it is perfectly certain that a fault has been committed, and always speak lovingly.

Never taunt with a mistake.

Never make a remark at the expense of each other.

Never part for a day without loving words to think of during absence.

Never meet without a loving welcome.

Never let the sun go down upon any anger or grievance.

Never let any fault you have committed go by until you have frankly confessed it and asked for forgiveness.

Never forget the happy hours of early love.

Never sigh over what might have been, but make the best of what is.

TOAST

May your joys be as bright as the morning, your years of happiness as numerous as the stars in the heavens, and your sorrows but shadows that fade in the sunlight of love.

Since the completion of the world God has been occupied joining couples.

RABBINIC SAYING

When two people in a dramatic service of divine worship extend open and defenseless hands and clasp them together, they are showing to God and to the world their readiness to learn from each other the mysterious penetration of real love.

ROBERT C. DODDS

The magic of marriage is that it creates meaningful goals to work for, struggle for, sacrifice for. It is the joint struggle that gives the relationship its meaning and keeps people alive.

HENRY GREGOR FELSEN

THE BRIDE

As slim and straight as the candles at her
    side
She stands, a flower with a flower's own
    grace.
Sheathed in the petaled satin of a bride,
Wrapped in a shimmering mist of fragile
    lace,
Serious and shy and very sweet,
She waits her lover's coming, eyes abrim
With happy dreams that are not yet
    complete
And only can be realized through him.

Here on the threshold of the years she
    stands,
So soon to leave her girlhood in the past.
God give her lover tender heart and hands
That the white radiance in her eyes may
    last;
God give her wisdom that she, too, may
    hold
His love till all the fires of earth grow cold.

GRACE NOLL CROWELL

ANALOGY

The beach is a marriage of sea and shore, a union of two different natures constantly interacting on each other. Every incoming wave affects the structure of the land, and as the land changes it affects the course and shape of the next wave. Where the land is sturdy rock, the alterations are minute and gradual. Years pass before a change is visible. If the shore is sand or fine pebbles, one gentle tide makes a noticeable difference and a violent storm may shift the whole beach. Then like a penitent spouse, the sea brings gifts, strewing the sloping littoral with shells, driftwood, seaweed bouquets— his tokens of reconciliation.

PRESBYTERIAN LIFE

Marriage is the most complete commitment of life, and as such should receive the best effort of all who enter into it. It must include willing work, sincere service, respect for each other, respect of self, humility and prayerfulness, and the healing power of love, and faith and common convictions— faith in God, faith in the future, and faith in the everlasting things of life. And to you who venture into marriage—and to you who have and to you who ever will— remember that respect and love and confidence must be earned every day, with encouragement and faithfulness and sincere consideration.

RICHARD L. EVANS

PRAYER FOR BRIDES AND GROOMS

May God send you
enough joy
to keep your hearts singing,
enough sorrow
to make you understanding,
enough hope to enrich your lives,
enough trials to keep you strong,
enough leisure
to refresh your spirits,
enough love
to make the world seem beautiful.

DINA DONOHUE

A BLESSING

Now you will feel no rain, for each
of you will be shelter for the other.
Now you will feel no cold, for each
of you will be warmth to the other.
Now there is no more loneliness.
Now you are two persons, but there
is one life before you.
Go now to your dwelling to enter
into the days of your life together.
And may your days be good, and long
upon the earth.

Two lives, belonging to different sexes, and often with widely different biological background, come together in the sight of God and before their friends to inaugurate something never seen in the world before— their particular combination of inheritance and their particular union of personalities.

ELTON TRUEBLOOD

A WEDDING HYMN

Jesus, stand beside them
  On this day of days,
That in happy wedlock
  They may live always.

Join their hands together,
  And their hearts make one;
Guard the troth now plighted
  And the life begun.

On their pleasant homestead
  Let Thy radiance rest;
Making joy and sorrow
  By Thy presence blest.

Gild their common duties
  With a light divine,
As, in Cana, water
  Thou didst change to wine.

Leave them nor forsake them;
  Ever be their Friend;
Guarding, guiding, blessing
  To their journey's end.

THOMAS TIPLADY

Marriage is a long conversation that always
seems too short!

ANDRE MAUROIS

RACHEL

Sunset, a flock of waiting sheep,
And Rachel beside the well;
Jacob, first beholding her,
Was bound within the spell
Of love more powerful than time.
No service he must pay
Could be too long—and seven years
Seemed but a day.

LESLIE SAVAGE CLARK

Whatever woman may cast her lot with
mine, should any ever do so, it is my inten-
tion to do all in my power to make her
happy and contented; and there is nothing I
can imagine that would make me more
unhappy than to fail in the effort.

ABRAHAM LINCOLN

O PERFECT LOVE

O perfect Love, all human thought
    transcending,
Lowly we kneel in prayer before Thy
    throne,
That theirs may be the love which knows no
    ending,
Whom thou forever more dost join in one.

O perfect Life, be Thou their full assurance
Of tender charity and steadfast faith,
Of patient hope, and quiet, brave
    endurance,
With child-like trust that fears nor pain nor
    death.

Grant them the joy which brightens earthly
    sorrow;
Grant them the peace which calms all
    earthly strife,
And to life's day the glorious unknown
    morrow
That dawns upon eternal love and life.

DOROTHY F. GURNEY

Here is the proper scene of piety and
patience, of the duty of parents, and the
charity of relatives; here kindness is spread
abroad, and love is united, and made firm
as a center: marriage is the nursery of
heaven.

JEREMY TAYLOR

Story writers say that love is concerned only with young people and the excitement and glamour of romance ends at the altar. How blind they are; the best romance is inside marriage; the finest love stories come after the wedding, not before.

IRVING STONE

There is no greater happiness
Than that of sharing life
With all its joys and all its cares
As loving man and wife.
For love gives life new meaning
And has a special way
Of growing stronger, deeper
With every passing day.
Yes, life is so much happier
And brighter when you're sharing
The very special joys that come
With loving ... giving ... caring.

BARBARA BURROW

WEDDING TRADITIONS

In olden days, a bride stood beneath a canopy to show she was under the protection of her groom. Nowadays she wears a wedding veil to symbolize her submission to him.

Because a circle is endless, a wedding ring is the symbol of undying love. The third finger left hand was chosen long ago when it was thought to be connected directly to the heart by the *vena amoris*, the vein of love.

The bride's garter is a good luck tradition begun in days of chivalry by the knights of the Order of the Garter. "Fate is sealed for the bachelor gay, when the bride's garter is tossed his way." The bride's bouquet has the same history.

When bride and groom share a piece of wedding cake, they break bread in kinship. The bride's knife signified the new wife's readiness to be keeper of her own household.

Toasting comes from the ancient French custom of putting bread in the bottom of the glass—a good toaster drained the drink to get the "toast." When bride and groom drink their wedding toast, legend says whoever finishes first will rule the family.

From earliest times newlyweds have been showered with the rice of abundance, while the bride's father threw her shoe after the groom, as a token of his surrender of his daughter.

From WEDDING-HYMN

May these two lives be but one note
  In the world's strange-sounding
    harmony,
Whose sacred music e'er shall float
  Through every discord up to Thee.

As when from separate stars two beams
  Unite to form one tender ray:
As when two sweet but shadowy dreams
  Explain each other in the day:

So may these two dear hearts one light
  Emit, and each interpret each.
Let an angel come and dwell to-night
  In this dear double-heart, and teach!

SIDNEY LANIER

When the one man loves the one woman and the one woman loves the one man, the very angels leave heaven and come and sit in that house and sing for joy.

BRAHMA

Marriages in the Family

_____ and _____

were joined in marriage by _____

on _____ at _____

_____ and _____

were joined in marriage by _____

on _____ at _____

_____ and _____

were joined in marriage by _____

on _____ at _____

_____ and _____

were joined in marriage by _____

on _____ at _____

_____ and _____

were joined in marriage by _____

on _____ at _____

_____ and _____

were joined in marriage by _____

on _____ at _____

Photographs

Building a Nest

BLESS THIS HOUSE

Bless this house, O Lord we pray,
  Make it safe by night and day.
Bless these walls, so firm and stout,
  Keeping want and trouble out;
Bless the roof and chimneys tall,
  Let Thy peace lie over all;
Bless this door, that it may prove
  Ever open to joy and love.

HELEN TAYLOR

A house is a home when it is put together
with a lot of promises, and love preserves it
as a sanctuary where those promises are
kept.

JAMES G. GOODWIN

PRAYER FOR A NEW HOUSE

May nothing evil cross this door,
  And may ill-fortune never pry
About these windows; may the roar
  And rains go by.

Strengthened by faith, these rafters will
  Withstand the battering of the storm;
This hearth, tho all the world grow chill,
  Will keep us warm.

Peace shall walk softly through these
    rooms,
  Touching our lips with holy wine.
Till every casual corner blooms
  Into a shrine.

Laughter shall drown the raucous shout;
  And, tho these sheltering walls are thin,
May they be strong to keep hate out
  And hold love in.

LOUIS UNTERMEYER

I bought a gay-roofed little house upon a
  sunny hill,
Where heaven is very close to earth and
  all the world is still.
It took my savings, every cent, although
  the cost was small,
But, oh, the lovely things I bought, and
  paid for not at all!
The sleepy valleys that below in tawny
  sunshine lie,
The oaks that sprawl across their slopes
  and climb to meet the sky,
Stray winds that sing of other things than
  those our eyes may see,
Blue wisps of mist, and raveled clouds that,
  fleeing, beckon me.
White suns of mad, glad April, October's
  wine to quaff,
On crystal winter mornings my hearth
  fire's crackling laugh,
The silent stars that march at night so
  close above my head,
The sound of raindrops on the roof when I
  am snug in bed.
For joist and beam and shingles gay I
  spent my savings small,
But on the lovely things God gave He put no
  price at all!

ROSE DARROUGH

DREAM HOUSE

Let there be within these phantom walls
Beauty where the hearth fire's shadow
    falls . . .
Quiet pictures—books—and welcoming
    chairs . . .
Music that the very silence shares . . .
Kitchen windows curtained blue and
    white . . .
Shelves and cupboards built for my
    delight . . .
Little things that lure and beckon me
With their tranquil joy! And let there be
Lilt of laughter—swift-forgotten tears
Woven through the fabric of the years . . .
Strength to guard me—eyes to answer
    mine,
Mutely clear. And though without may
    shine
Stars of dawn or sunset's wistful glow—
All of life and love my house shall know!

           CATHERINE PARMENTER NEWELL

There are two heavens,
Both made of love—one inconceivable
Ev'n by the other, so divine it is;
The other, far on this side of the stars,
By men called home.

           LEIGH HUNT

THE HOMEMAKER'S CREED

I believe in the divine origin of the home; that it was given to man and woman to enable them to comprehend the love of God and to glimpse the heaven beyond.

I believe in the love of one man for one woman; of parents for their children; of the family for the lonely wanderer who crosses the threshold.

I believe in the companionship of the home; the comradeship of husband and wife; of father and son; of mother and daughter.

I believe in the sanctity of the home; that it should be a sacred and peaceful garden from which the busy-body, the meddler, and the sounder of discords should be fenced out.

I believe in the hospitality of the home; that its doors should swing wide to true friends, to wayfarers and to those who walk alone.

I believe in the influence of the home, that it should ally itself with the great organizations which are advancing the cause of humanity.

I believe in the home which has a place for the boy or girl where they may bring friends without reproof; where they may collect materials or start an aquarium; where the call to home pleasures is louder than the lure of the streets.

           NEW CENTURY LEADER

DEDICATION

O Thou whose gracious presence blest
  The home at Bethany,
This shelter from the world's unrest,
This home made ready for its Guest,
We dedicate to Thee.

We build an altar here, and pray
  That Thou wilt show Thy face.
Dear Lord, if Thou wilt come to stay,
This home we consecrate today
Will be a holy place.

LOUIS F. BENSON

A flowered shrine within a friendly town
Where one can lose the world and be at
      peace
Beneath the trees, or puttering in the sun—
Or watch the pageantry of fiery fleece
Against the skyline when the day is done.
A modest plot, but one we call our own.

Together, we have dreamed it into being—
Watched o'er its building till it stood at last
Smiling in welcome, perfect in our sight.
It took us to its hearth and held us fast
To guard our life and love by day and
      night—
Safe haven now and far beyond our seeing.

No other place can ever hold, for me,
The garnered treasure of these fruitful
      years—
That you and I, my dear, are living through.
Whether they bring us joy or pain and tears
Within these walls I share it all with you
And catch an echo of God's symphony.

R. K. FLETCHER

Take what God gives, O heart of mine,
  And build your house of happiness.
Perchance some have been given more;
  But many have been given less.
The treasure lying at your feet,
  Whose value you but faintly guess,
Another builder, looking on,
  Would barter heaven to possess.

B. Y. WILLIAMS

Every day we live presents opportunities for adventure. A beautiful view, a fragrant flower, a little trip to another town, an unexpected letter, a joyful reunion with a friend. All of these commonplace experiences, and many more, make up the warp and woof from which the fabric of our daily life existence is woven.

Home in one form or another, is the great object of life.

JOSIAH GILBERT HOLLAND

HOUSE BLESSING

Bless the four corners of this house,
   And be the lintel blest;
And bless the hearth and bless the board
   And bless each place of rest;
And bless the door that opens wide
   To stranger as to kin;
And bless each crystal window-pane
   That lets the starlight in;
And bless the rooftree overhead
   And every sturdy wall,
The peace of man, the peace of God,
   The peace of Love on all!

ARTHUR GUITERMAN

With gratitude for all that Christian homes and family life have meant and can mean, we dedicate our hearts and homes to Thee. We dedicate them to the intelligence of love, the strength of faith, the gladness of beauty, and the nobility of reverence. We dedicate them to thoughts that make us pure, to hopes that make us brave, to trust that makes us serene. We dedicate them to hospitality which strengthens friendship and joy, to humility which builds bridges of understanding, and releases the saving grandeur of forgiveness.

EVERETT W. PALMER

DEFINITIONS

Home is a world of strife shut out, a world of love shut in.

Home is a father's kingdom, a mother's world, and the children's paradise.

Home is a place where our stomachs get three square meals a day, and our hearts a thousand.

A Child Is Born

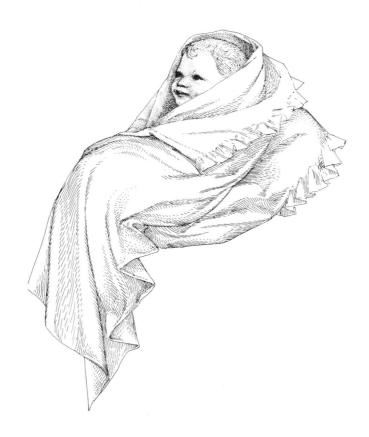

A PRAYER WHEN A CHILD IS BORN

O God, the Source from which we all have come, we thank Thee for this sign that Thou art not discouraged with the world: a child has been born. We praise Thee for every new-born babe, for every new commingling of the Divine with our dust, and especially for this child, this bright little horizon where earth and Heaven meet.

Bless him this day and all his days. In his infancy may he be quietly aware of the love that nurtures and shelters him. Let each day move him from helpless babyhood toward helpful manhood. May the highest ideals and noblest purposes be transplanted from his parents' hearts and minds to his fertile character; there may they grow and be fruitful.

Grant him a curious and appreciative interest in the world around him, a zest for life, and a passion for goodness. Give him both grace of bearing and beauty in the inner man. Stretch his mind and heart to make room for Thee and a place for all mankind, and let him become like the Boy of Nazareth who "increased in wisdom and stature, and in favor with God and man."

HAROLD E. KOHN

From SURPRISED BY LIGHT

To be
is miracle enough.
To sense that I am,
here,
in this time,
in this space,
so unique and special.
One day I appeared on this earth
and said: I am I.
That is miracle enough.

ULRICH SCHAFFER

MOTHERHOOD

A sudden grown-up feeling at the first pulse of life within you.

A surge of joy and tenderness at a baby's first cry.

An aching back after housework is done, formulas made, and baby is bathed and fed.

Watching him grow, thrilling at his first smile, his first word, his first step alone.

Caring for him through long sleepless nights of pain.

Teaching him how to walk and talk and telling him about God and His wonders.

Parting with him when he starts to school.

Mending torn clothing and buying new shoes for feet that grow too fast.

Taking him to the dentist.

Staying at his bedside and being there when he wakes up from his operation.

Sharing enthusiasm over his efforts to achieve and having pride in his success.

Being tolerant of his adolescent traits and being kind to his friends.

Helping him choose his graduation suit.

Praying with an aching heart when he's gone overseas.

Feeling joy and thankfulness at his safe return.

Sharing excitement and happiness at his wedding.

Relaxing in contentment—now that you're grandma.

IOLA M. ANDERSON

When the first baby laughed for the first time, the laugh broke into a million pieces, and they all went skipping about. That was the beginning of fairies.

JAMES M. BARRIE

Life is a flame that is always burning itself out, but it catches fire again every time a child is born.

GEORGE BERNARD SHAW

MESSAGE FROM GOD

When God wants an important thing done in this world or a wrong righted, he goes about it in a very singular way. He doesn't release his thunderbolts or stir up his earthquakes. He simply has a tiny baby born, perhaps in a very humble home, perhaps of a very humble mother. And he puts the idea or purpose into the mother's heart. And she puts it in the baby's mind, and then—God waits. The great events of this world are not battles and elections and earthquakes and thunderbolts. The great events are babies, for each child comes with the message that God is not yet discouraged with man but is still expecting goodwill to become incarnate in each human life.

EDWARD McDONALD

MIRACLE

Close-hung with silence was the room;
Through starlit distances there came to
 earth
A thread from off God's never ceasing loom;
And mortals knew—the miracle of birth.

No painter has ever been able perfectly to reproduce the picture of the mother holding in her arms her babe.

WILLIAM JENNINGS BRYAN

CHRISTMAS LULLABY

Sleep, my baby, gently slumber,
 While the snowflakes fall:
God Himself was once a baby,
 Cradled in a stall.

Sleep, my baby, gently slumber,
 Dark the night, and cold;
We will warm it with a story,
 Sweetest ever told.

Sleep, my baby, gently slumber,
 Blessed Jesus cares:
He who was Himself a baby
 Hears a baby's prayers.

Sleep, my baby, gently slumber,
 Jesus understands.
Oh, the love that God has proffered
 In a Baby's hands!

HELEN FRAZEE-BOWER

When the first Mother awoke to her first tenderness and warmed her loneliness at her infant's love, when for a moment she forgot herself and thought upon its weakness or its pain, when by the most imperceptible act or sign or look of sympathy she expressed the unutterable impulse of her Motherhood, the touch of a new creative hand was felt upon the world. However short the earliest infancies, however feeble the sparks they fanned, however long heredity took to gather fuel enough for a steady flame, it is certain that once this fire began to warm the cold hearth of Nature and give humanity a heart, the most stupendous task of the past was accomplished.

HENRY DRUMMOND

Mother Love

BEING A MOTHER

Being a Mother is helping with his homework, only to be told, "That isn't the way my teacher does it." It's report cards, good and bad, and P.T.A., and graduations. It is six Cub Scouts in the kitchen, pounding nails into bookends—you hope—that they are making for Mother's Day gifts. It is putting up curls and letting down hems for long-legged little girls.

It is teaching little ones to ask the blessing at meals, then hearing the same childish prayer for years. It is rushing around on Sunday morning, preparing breakfast and dinner at the same time, serving breakfast, rinsing and stacking the dishes, then getting ready for Sunday School in five minutes flat, only to find that one of the children is calmly reading the funnies and hasn't quite managed to put on his shoes and socks.

Being a Mother brings long conferences and arguments, with father. It involves long nights in prayer, and literally thousands of short, wordless prayers that you just know God understands.

Being a Mother is being demoted to the back seat when the children learn to drive, and lying wakefully waiting for them to come in from a date, then falling asleep in the thirty seconds that elapse between the locking of the front door and the goodnight kiss. It is feeling like Queen Victoria when a roomful of your son's friends, suddenly young men, jump to their feet as you enter the room.

Being a Mother is loving, praying, doing, as long as children, any children, need affection, genuine interest, physical care, and spiritual guidance.

VIRGINIA GABLE

MY MOTHER

I walk upon the rocky shore,
Her strength is in the ocean's roar.
I glance into the shaded pool,
Her mind is there so calm and cool.

I hear sweet rippling of the sea,
Naught but her laughter 'tis to me.
I gaze into the starry skies,
And there I see her wondrous eyes.

I look into my inmost mind,
And here her inspiration find.
In all I am and hear and see,
My precious mother is with me.

JOSEPHINE RICE CREELMAN

Who ran to help me when I fell,
And would some pretty story tell,
Or kiss the place to make it well?
    My mother.

JANE TAYLOR

Mother is the name for God in the lips and hearts of little children.

WILLIAM MAKEPEACE THACKERAY

WHAT IS A MOTHER?

A mother is a person who is old enough to be an authority on Indian war whoops and whether cowboys ever went barefoot, and yet young enough to remember the rules of the game May I? and the second verse of Sing a Song of Sixpence.

She must not only be an expert laundress, but always remember to remove sand and pebbles and string from pockets; and she must be a seamstress and adept at sewing on buttons, letting down and taking up sleeves and pants legs and able to patch threadbare corduroy knees so the patches do not show.

She must be a doctor and able to remove splinters without hurting, stop bleeding noses, vaporize colds, read stories to measle-speckled boys, and always have on hand an endless supply of ready-cut bandages.

She must be a magician and keep a bottomless cooky jar, a constant supply of apples in the refrigerator, and be able instantly to recognize a scribbled drawing as a beautiful picture of a man walking down a dirt road with a pan on his head.

She must be able to balance a baby under one arm, a small boy climbing up her back and another trying to tie her feet into knots, and still write a check for the dry cleaners.

A mother is a queer sort of person. In a single instant her endless cooking and dishwashing and ironing and sock darning and knee bandaging can swell over into a heart-thrilling wave of pride on visitors' day at the kindergarten when Mike stands up in his new red sweater, replies "Yes, ma'am" to the teacher, and solemnly walks to the front of the room to direct the rhythm band.

A mother's payment is rich and full, but often comes in little ways: a wadded bouquet of dandelion puffs; seeing Greg, unnoticed, share his tricycle with the new little boy across the street; watching Brian reach to pluck a neighbor's prize tulip . . . hold his hand in mid-air a second . . . and then toddle off to chase a butterfly. Her payment comes in the cherished words of a small boy's prayers at night when Mike adds a P.S. to God to "also bless Billy even though he pushed me off the swing today."

Then a mother kisses three blond heads, turns off the light and hugs a smile to her heart as she walks downstairs. And after the dishes are done, before she gets out her mending box, she puts a batch of cookies in the oven for a surprise tomorrow.

NAN CARROLL

DEFINITION

I search among the plain and lovely words
To find what one word "Mother" means; as
    well
Try to define the tangled song of birds;
The echo in the hills of one clear bell.
One cannot snare the wind, or catch the
    wings
Of shadows flying low across the wheat;
Ah, who can prison simple, natural things
That make the long days beautiful and
    sweet?

Mother—a word that holds the tender spell
Of all the dear essential things of earth;
A home, clean sunlit rooms, and the good
    smell
Of Bread; a table spread; a glowing hearth.
And love beyond the dream of anyone . . .
I search for words for her . . . and there are
    none.

GRACE NOLL CROWELL

From DEAR OLD MOTHERS

I love old mothers—mothers with white
    hair
    And kindly eyes, and lips grown soft and
      sweet
With murmured blessings over sleeping
    babes.
    There is something in their quiet grace
That speaks the calm of Sabbath
    afternoons;
    A knowledge in their deep, unfaltering
      eyes
That far outreaches all philosophy.

CHARLES S. ROSS

From THE PRINCESS

    I love her, one
Not learned, save in gracious household
    ways,
Not perfect, nay, but full of tender wants,
No angel, but a dearer being, all dipt
In angel instincts, breathing Paradise,
Interpreter between the gods and men,
Who look'd all native to her place, and yet
On tiptoe seem'd to touch upon a sphere
Too gross to tread, and all male minds
    perforce
Sway'd to her from their orbits as they
    moved,
And girdled her with music. Happy he
With such a mother! faith in womankind
Beats in his blood, and trust in all things
    high
Comes easy to him, and tho' he trip and fall
He shall not blind his soul with clay.

ALFRED LORD TENNYSON

A good mother is the equal of a dozen school teachers, a small convention of clergymen, and a score of policemen and judges, all added together. A mother is a Jacquelyn-of-all-trades. She is a singer, whose hymns crooned at the cradle and sung at the ironing board and the kitchen sink will, like God's goodness and mercy, follow us all the days of our lives. She preaches sermons one can see, as well as hear, by the way she walks happily through our lives. She models, and womanhood looks good on her. She is an interpreter who knows the precise meaning of a baby's cry, a boy's anguished yelp, a daughter's sob, or a husband's scowl, and she comes on the run with the exact answer.

Mother is a clever magician, adroitly changing life's heaviest drudgery into life's highest privilege, making ordinary sons look like heroes and transforming ordinary daughters into radiant angels by waving a word of praise. With a reassuring word she makes childhood worries disappear into thin air, and with a touch of her hand she changes a child's chaos to calmness. With her softly spoken prayer the air is cleared of anger and ill-will, and all our sin-soiled world seems bright and good again.

HAROLD E. KOHN

LIKENESSES

I know what mother's face is like,
    Although I cannot see;
It's like the music of a bell;
It's like the roses I can smell—
    Yes, these it's like to me.

I know what father's face is like;
    I'm sure I know it all;
It's like his whistle on the air;
It's like his arms which take such care
    And never let me fall.

And I can tell what God is like—
    The God whom no one sees.
He's everything my parents seem;
He's fairer than my fondest dream,
    And greater than all these.

From MY MOTHER'S WORDS

My mother has the prettiest tricks
    Of words and words and words.
Her talk comes out as smooth and sleek
    As breasts of singing birds.

She shapes her speech all silver fine
    Because she loves it so.
And her own eyes begin to shine
    To hear her stories grow.

And if she goes to make a call
    Or out to take a walk,
We leave our work when she returns
    And run to hear her talk.

ANNA HEMPSTEAD BRANCH

A mother can be almost any size or any age, but she won't admit to anything over thirty. A mother has soft hands and smells good. A mother likes new dresses, music, a clean house, her children's kisses, an automatic washer and Daddy.

A mother doesn't like having her children sick, muddy feet, temper tantrums, loud noise or bad report cards. A mother can read a thermometer (much to the amazement of Daddy) and like magic, can kiss a hurt away.

A mother can bake good cakes and pies but likes to see her children eat vegetables. A mother can stuff a fat baby into a snow suit in seconds and can kiss sad little faces and make them smile.

A mother is underpaid, has long hours and gets very little rest. She worries too much about her children, but she says she doesn't mind at all. And no matter how old her children are, she still likes to think of them as her little babies.

She is the guardian angel of the family, the queen, the tender hand of love.

Wife's Family Tree

FATHER

DATE BORN

PLACE

BROTHERS, SISTERS

NAME

DATE BORN

PLACE

BROTHERS, SISTERS

MOTHER

DATE BORN

PLACE

BROTHERS, SISTERS

	FATHER
FATHER	DATE BORN
	PLACE
DATE BORN	BROTHERS, SISTERS
PLACE	MOTHER
	DATE BORN
BROTHERS, SISTERS	PLACE
	BROTHERS, SISTERS
MOTHER	FATHER
	DATE BORN
DATE BORN	PLACE
	BROTHERS, SISTERS
PLACE	
	MOTHER
BROTHERS, SISTERS	DATE BORN
	PLACE
	BROTHERS, SISTERS
FATHER	FATHER
	DATE BORN
DATE BORN	PLACE
	BROTHERS, SISTERS
PLACE	
	MOTHER
BROTHERS, SISTERS	DATE BORN
	PLACE
	BROTHERS, SISTERS
MOTHER	FATHER
	DATE BORN
DATE BORN	PLACE
	BROTHERS, SISTERS
PLACE	
	MOTHER
BROTHERS, SISTERS	DATE BORN
	PLACE
	BROTHERS, SISTERS

Daddy's Home

A FATHER PRAYS

Lord, who am I to teach the way
To this dear child from day to day,
So prone myself to go astray?
I teach her power to will and do,
But in the teaching learn anew
My own great weakness through and
    through.
I teach her love for all mankind
And all God's creatures, but I find
My love comes lagging far behind.
Lord, if her guide I still must be,
Oh, may this child so dear to me
See I am leaning hard on Thee.

LESLIE PINCKNEY HILL

THE JOYS OF BEING A FATHER

To watch her tumble into bed
  After she's had her story read;
To have her climb onto my lap,
  And snuggle close to take her nap;
To know that in her eyes I stand
  As tall and strong as any man;
To teach her how to do what's right,
  To hear her ask how stars give light;
To know she'll bring me all her fears,
  Because she knows I'll dry her tears;
To watch her sleep with rumpled hair,
  To see her scold her teddy bear;
To see her dressed in mommy's clothes,
  To watch her smell her first spring rose;
To feel her gentle, loving touch
  As she holds the hand she trusts so much;
To share the things that make her sad,
  To hear her say, "I love you, dad";
To scold and then to see her pout,
  To help her learn what life's about;
My lovely princess, as only she can,
  Makes me glad I'm a father and a man.

J. DENNIS SHIELDS

FATHER AND DAD

A father sends his child to church; a dad goes with him.

A father buys you your first two-wheeler bike; a dad runs along with you when you try to ride it.

A father never misses a golf date; a dad gets it off the roof for you.

A father remembers your birthday; a dad remembers what you got in Spanish last semester.

A father wants you to make the basket-ball team; a dad knows you're better off if you don't.

A father is happy if you are popular; a dad is happy if you wash the car.

A father looks nifty in a tuxedo; a dad cries at your wedding.

A father is nothing more than a biological entity, a male parent; a dad is the guy who loves you.

JAN COMPTON

WHAT FATHER TEACHES

He teaches kindness—by being thoughtful and gracious even at home.

He teaches patience—by being gentle and understanding over and over.

He teaches honesty—by keeping his promises to his family even when it costs.

He teaches courage—by living unafraid, with faith, in all circumstances.

He teaches justice—by being fair and dealing equally with everyone.

We never know the love of the parent till we become parents ourselves.

HENRY WARD BEECHER

A father is many things to his child. As a teacher, he helps us learn valuable lessons about God's law and purpose. As a guide, he sets a pattern for life—for the ideals we should embrace and the goals we should seek. As a companion, he provides that close friendship God wishes every young person to enjoy. It is, indeed, through the influence of a father on earth that we better know and understand our Father in heaven.

JAMES KELLER

TRIBUTE TO A FOSTER FATHER

Because he lived, I had a home and love,
A light to guide when days were dark and
    there were clouds above.
I had the warmth, the food, the clothes,
    a hand to hold when skies were overcast
    and it was cold.

I had a strength on which my childish
    faith could lean,
And I could dare to hope and, with his
    help, fulfill a cherished dream.

I thank thee, Heavenly Father, for this
    gift that small lads need and crave:
An earthly father's love and care,
    and these, he gave.

RUBY A. JONES

Father is one of the most wonderful of all words in our language. We give thanks for our earthly father; for the father of our country, George Washington; for our spiritual father, Abraham, the man of faith; and for our Heavenly Father.

MERRITT W. FAULKNER

Who has not carolled Mary,
    And who her praise would dim?
But what of humble Joseph:
    Is there no song for him?

If Joseph had not driven
    Straight nails through honest wood;
If Joseph had not cherished
    His Mary as he should;

If Joseph had not proved him
    A sire both kind and wise
Would he have drawn with favour
    The Child's all-probing eyes?

Would Christ have prayed "Our Father,"
    Or cried that Name in death,
Unless he first had honoured
    Joseph of Nazareth?

GILBERT THOMAS

ECHOES

What a father says to his children is not heard by the world, but it will be heard by posterity.

JEAN PAUL RICHTER

Husband's Family Tree

FATHER

DATE BORN

PLACE

BROTHERS, SISTERS

NAME

DATE BORN

PLACE

BROTHERS, SISTERS

MOTHER

DATE BORN

PLACE

BROTHERS, SISTERS

	FATHER
	DATE BORN
FATHER	PLACE
	BROTHERS, SISTERS
DATE BORN	
	MOTHER
PLACE	DATE BORN
	PLACE
BROTHERS, SISTERS	BROTHERS, SISTERS
	FATHER
MOTHER	DATE BORN
	PLACE
DATE BORN	BROTHERS, SISTERS
PLACE	MOTHER
	DATE BORN
BROTHERS, SISTERS	PLACE
	BROTHERS, SISTERS
	FATHER
FATHER	DATE BORN
	PLACE
DATE BORN	BROTHERS, SISTERS
PLACE	MOTHER
	DATE BORN
BROTHERS, SISTERS	PLACE
	BROTHERS, SISTERS
MOTHER	
	FATHER
DATE BORN	DATE BORN
	PLACE
	BROTHERS, SISTERS
PLACE	
	MOTHER
BROTHERS, SISTERS	DATE BORN
	PLACE
	BROTHERS, SISTERS

It's the Little Things That Count

Jesus, teach me how to be
Gracious in simplicity.

Sweep the floors, wash the clothes,
Gather for each vase a rose.

Iron and mend a tiny frock,
Keeping one eye on the clock.

Always having time kept free
For childish questions asked of me.

Grant me wisdom Mary had
When she taught her little lad.

CATHERINE C. COBLENTZ

You are richer today than you were yesterday if you have laughed often, given something, forgiven even more, made a new
friend, or made stepping stones of stum-
bling blocks.

You are richer today than you were yesterday if you have thought more in terms of
thyself than myself or if you have managed
to be cheerful even if you were weary.

You are richer tonight than you were this
morning if you have taken time to trace the
handiwork of God in the commonplace
things of life, if you have learned to count
out things that really don't count, or if you
have been a little blinder to the faults of
friend or foe.

You are richer if a little child has smiled
at you and a stray dog has licked your hand
or if you have looked for the best in others
and have given others the best in you.

LOIS MAE CUHEL

THE COMMON TASKS

The common tasks are beautiful if we
Have eyes to see their shining ministry.
The plowman with his share deep in the
     loam,
The carpenter whose skilled hands build a
     home,
The gardener working with reluctant sod,
Faithful to his partnership with God—
These are the artisans of life, and oh,
A woman with her eyes and cheeks aglow,
Watching a kettle, tending a scarlet flame,
Guarding a little child—there is no name
For these great ministries, and eyes are dull
That do not see that they are beautiful,
That do not see within the common tasks
The simple answer to the thing God asks
Of any child, a pride within His breast:
That at our given work we do our best.

GRACE NOLL CROWELL

COMMONPLACES

"A commonplace life," we say, and we sigh;
But why should we sigh as we say?
The commonplace sun in the commonplace
     sky,
Makes up the commonplace day;
The moon and the stars are commonplace
     things,
And the flower that blooms, and the bird
     that sings:
But dark were the world and sad our lot
If the flowers failed and the bird sang not;
And God, who studies each separate soul
Of our commonplace lives makes His
     beautiful whole.

SUSAN COOLIDGE

SPRING-CLEANING NOTES

Oil a dream and make it work.
Polish my heart until love glows.
Clean out basement where fears lurk.
Mend complaining where it shows.
Tighten hinge on self-control.
Wash the window of my soul.

JESSIE MERLE FRANKLIN

HEART AND HANDS

In Martha's kitchen ministry
And Mary's better choice I see
A deep desire to serve and praise
Expressed in two essential ways.

To harmonize these ways demands
Perceptive use of heart and hands
To emulate the Mary good
Yet share the Martha sisterhood.

FLORENCE PEDIGO JANSSON

From HOME

Each morn
When I go forth upon the duties of the day
I wend my way
Content to know that eve will bring me
Safely to thy walls again.

NELLIE WOMACK HINES

It is in the family where human beings can best fulfill their needs of intimacy, personal development, and self-identity. The more impersonal the rest of the world becomes the more these needs will be fulfilled by the family.

LOUIS E. GELINEAU

A MOTHER'S MORNING PRAYER

Good morning, Lord.
Another day has begun,
Though the stars have not paled
To the morning sun.
Forgive me, Lord,
If I meditate
With one eye on the clock
So I won't be late.
There's bacon to fry,
And eggs to fix,
And lunches to pack
Though it's only six.
My family still sleeps
Without worry or care,
Assured in their minds
That I'll be there
To wake them each morning;
Then send on their way,
Hopefully prepared
To meet the day.
Thank you, Lord,
For my children, three;
And my deep awareness
That they need me.
Oh, dear Lord,
I do earnestly pray
That I'll listen to you
As I face this day.
I must hurry now,
The east glows red
And my rising family
Must be fed.
I know they are Yours
To have and hold,
But may night find them
Safe in my fold.

BETTY H. BROWN

STATISTICS

A mother will probably do the following for one child:

Wash and fold 17,520 diapers, give or take a few.

Prepare for one child 19,710 meals, that's for eighteen years; slightly fewer if you can throw in a few hamburgers and fried chicken from the carry-out restaurants.

Scrub the grass stain from 5,970 pairs of blue jeans.

Sew on 456 buttons.

Remove 37 wads of bubble gum.

Insist upon 5,970 baths.

Supervise homework for 1,620 nights.

Endure 520 Saturdays of Magilla Gorilla and the Jackson Five cartoons until such time as the interest shifts to Saturday afternoons of football, hockey, and baseball games.

If you are the mother of a girl you will probably try to find 27 lost barrettes, mend 35 slip straps, buy 150 pairs of hose, suffer through four or five romances, and get through a wedding without weeping.

If you should have more than one child, multiply these figures by the number of children you have, and in addition you will settle at least 500 arguments a year for as long as you have two or more children at home.

You can add to the above figures, 365 goodnight kisses each year. Count on just about ten years for boys, slightly longer for girls, who may forget the goodnight ritual if they are engrossed in hearing their favorite singer croon.

Add the joys of holding that tiny new baby in your arms, the pride of watching him in his first school play, seeing him hit a home run in Little League, hearing her play a piano solo for the spring recital, sharing the happiness of Mother's Day and the excitement of many Christmases.

ANNE ROBINSON HUGHES

A MOTHER'S PRAYER

Father in Heaven, make me wise,
  So that my gaze may never meet
A question in my children's eyes.
  God keep me always kind and sweet,

And patient, too, before their need;
  Let each vexation know its place,
Let gentleness be all my creed,
  Let laughter live upon my face!

A mother's day is very long,
  There are so many things to do!
But never let me lose my song
  Before the hardest day is through.

MARGARET E. SANGSTER

BEATITUDES FOR A HOUSEWIFE

Blessed is she whose daily tasks are a labor of love, for she translates duty into privilege.

Blessed is she who mends stockings and toys and broken hearts, for her understanding is a balm to humanity.

Blessed is she who serves laughter and smiles at every meal, for she shall be blessed with goodness.

Blessed is she who preserves the sanctity of the Christian home, for hers is a sacred trust that crowns her with dignity.

Father, I scarcely dare to pray,
    So clear I see, now it is done,
That I have wasted half my day,
    And left my work but just begun;

So clear I see that things I thought
    Were right or harmless were a sin;
So clear I see that I have sought,
    Unconscious, selfish aims to win;

So clear I see that I have hurt
    The souls I might have helped to save;
That I have slothful been, inert,
    Deaf to the calls thy leaders gave.

In outskirts of thy kingdoms vast,
    Father, the humblest spot give me;
Set me the lowliest task thou hast;
    Let me repentent work for thee.

                    HELEN HUNT JACKSON

Life is not made up of great sacrifices and
duties, but of little things; in which smiles
and kindness and small obligations, given
habitually, are what win and preserve the
heart and secure comfort.

                    SIR HUMPHREY DAVY

HIGHWAYS OF HAPPINESS

Take time to look. It is the price of success.
    Take time to think. It is a source of power.
    Take time to play. It is the secret of perennial youth.
    Take time to read. It is the source of wisdom.
    Take time to be friendly. It is the way to happiness.
    Take time to laugh. It is the music of the soul.

The madonnas I see are those that pass the
house on the way to work, carrying little
saviors in their arms.

                    MARGARET T. APPLEGARTH

New every morning is the love
    Our wakening and uprising prove;
Through sleep and darkness safely brought,
    Restored to life and power and thought.

The trivial round, the common task,
    Will furnish all we ought to ask;
Room to deny ourselves—a road
    To bring us daily nearer God.

                    JOHN KEBLE

The best combination of parents consists of
a father who is gentle beneath his firmness
and a mother who is firm beneath her
gentleness.

                    SYDNEY J. HARRIS

Bedtime

I do not know of a better shrine before which a father or mother may kneel or stand than that of a sleeping child. I do not know of a holier place, a temple where one is more likely to come into closer touch with all that is infinitely good, where one may come nearer to seeing and feeling God. From that shrine come matins of love and laughter, of trust and cheer to bless the new day; and before that shrine should fall our soft vespers, our grateful benedictions for the night. At the cot of a sleeping babe all man-made ranks and inequalities are ironed out, and all mankind kneels reverently before the living image of the Creator.

JUSTICE W. McEACHREN

Sweet it is to fall asleep in one's own home, in the familiar bed, under the quilt worked by loving hands, perhaps a dear nurse's hands, those kind, tender, untiring hands.

IVAN TURGENEV

AT BEDTIME

Matthew, Mark, Luke and John
Bless the bed that I lie on!
Four corners to my bed,
Four angels round my head,
One at head and one at feet,
And two to guard my soul asleep.

A DUTCH LULLABY

Wynken, Blynken, and Nod one night
  Sailed off in a wooden shoe,—
Sailed on a river of crystal light
  Into a sea of dew.
"Where are you going, and what do you
    wish?"
  The old moon asked the three.
"We have come to fish for the herring fish
  That live in this beautiful sea;
  Nets of silver and gold have we!"
    Said Wynken,
    Blynken,
    And Nod.

The old moon laughed and sang a song,
  As they rocked in the wooden shoe;
And the wind that sped them all night long
  Ruffled the waves of dew.
The little stars were the herring fish
  That lived in that beautiful sea—
"Now cast your nets wherever you wish,—
  Never afeared are we!"
So cried the stars to the fishermen three,
    Wynken,
    Blynken,
    And Nod.

All night long their nets they threw
  To the stars in the twinkling foam,—
Then down from the skies came the wooden
    shoe,
  Bringing the fishermen home:
'Twas all so pretty a sail, it seemed
  As if it could not be;
And some folk thought 'twas a dream
    they'd dreamed
  Of sailing that beautiful sea;
But I shall name you the fishermen three:
    Wynken,
    Blynken,
    And Nod.

EUGENE FIELD

Wee Willie Winkie runs through the town,
Upstairs and downstairs in his nightgown,
Rapping at the window, crying through the
    lock,
"Are the children in their beds, for now it's
    eight o'clock?"

MOTHER GOOSE

WHILE WE PRAY

The shadows of the evening hours
Fall from the darkening sky;
Upon the fragrance of the flowers
The dews of evening lie:
Before Thy throne, O Lord of heaven,
We kneel at close of day;
Look on Thy children from on high,
And hear us while we pray.

Slowly the rays of daylight fade:
So fade within our heart
The hopes in earthly love and joy,
That one by one depart.
Slowly the bright stars, one by one
Within the heavens shine:
Give us, O Lord, fresh hopes in heav'n,
And trust in things divine.

Let peace, O Lord, Thy peace, O God,
Upon our souls descend;
From midnight fears and perils, Thou
Our trembling hearts defend.
Give us a respite from our toil,
Calm and subdue our woes;
Through the long day we labor, Lord,
O give us now repose.

ADELAIDE A. PROCTER

BLANKETS

A child will clutch an old blanket or an old and battered toy, and will not let it go. He takes it with him to bed, as though it were his most priceless possession. The blanket is precious precisely because it is old and worn, because around it cluster many sweet memories of being tucked into it by the tender and loving hands of mother, night after night. The blanket is an anchor that holds the tiny ship to the shore, while yet permitting it to venture a little way in slow motions of discovery and exploration.

We all clutch old blankets of one kind or another. We feel a special attachment to objects, and places, and people, because they carry happy memories for us. We hold on to ideas and persist in habits because they carry the compulsion of the familiar.

BEN ZION BOKSER

BED IN SUMMERTIME

In winter I get up at night
And dress by yellow candle-light
In summer, quite the other way,
I have to go to bed by day.

I have to go to bed and see
The birds still hopping on the tree,
Or hear the grown-up people's feet
Still going past me in the street.

And does it not seem hard to you,
When all the sky is clear and blue,
And I should like so much to play,
To have to go to bed by day?

ROBERT LOUIS STEVENSON

LITTLE JESUS

Little Jesus, was Thou shy
Once, and just as small as I?
And what did it feel like to be
Out of Heaven, and just like me?

And did Thy Mother at the night
Kiss Thee and fold the clothes in right?
And didst Thou feel quite good in bed,
Kissed, and sweet, and Thy prayers said?

FRANCIS THOMPSON

From THE SUGAR-PLUM TREE

Have you ever heard of the Sugar-Plum
    Tree?
'Tis a marvel of great renown!
It blooms on the shore of the Lollypop Sea
In the garden of Shut-Eye Town;
The fruit that it bears is so wondrously
    sweet
(As those who have tasted it say)
That good little children have only to eat
Of that fruit to be happy next day.

There are marshmallows, gumdrops, and
    peppermint canes
With stripings of scarlet and gold,
And you carry away of the treasure that
    rains,
As much as your apron can hold!
So come, little child, cuddle closer to me
In your dainty white nightcap and gown,
And I'll rock you away to that Sugar-Plum
    Tree
In the garden of Shut-Eye Town.

EUGENE FIELD

MOTHER'S LOVE

Her love is like an island
    In life's ocean, vast and wide,
A peaceful, quiet shelter
    From the wind, and rain, and tide.

'Tis bound on the north by Hope,
    By Patience on the west,
By tender Counsel on the south,
    And on the east by Rest.

Above it like a beacon light
    Shine faith, and truth, and prayer;
And through the changing scenes of life,
    I find a haven there.

PRAYER AT BEDTIME

Here in the dusk I watch them kneel to
    pray,
    And all the gratitude I cannot speak
And all the loving words I long to say
    Are written in the tears upon my cheek.
How can I thank thee, Lord, for such as
    these,
    This blessed heritage vouchsafed to me—
My children, confident, upon their knees,
    Their simple faith, their hushed
        expectancy?

Oh, I will open wide the sacred book
    And speak to them of all thy matchless
        grace;
So shall they come, in infancy, to look
    Beyond all other faces to thy face.
Yes, I will share the treasures of thy Word
    With these. I cannot thank thee better,
        Lord.

HELEN FRAZEE-BOWER

GOOD NIGHT

On tip-toe comes the gentle dark
To help the children sleep
And silently, in silver paths,
The slumber fairies creep.

Then overhead, God sees that all
His candles are a-light
And reaching loving arms to us
He bids His world Good Night.

DOROTHY MASON PIERCE

LULLABY

Bye low, bye, baby bye,
Sun is gone, night is come now.
Bye low, bye low, baby bye,
Birds and flow'rs have closed their eyes.
On the grass shadows lie,
Bye low, bye, baby bye.
On the grass shadows lie,
Bye low, bye, baby bye.

Bye low, bye, baby bye,
One by one stars are peeping.
Bye low, bye low, baby bye,
In the nighttime sky they shine,
While the moon floats above,
Bye low, bye, baby bye.
While the moon floats above,
Bye low, bye, baby bye.

Bye low, bye, baby bye,
Mother tenderly holds thee.
Bye low, bye low, baby bye,
May the Lord God bless thy rest.
Bye low, bye, baby bye,
Angels guard thee in sleep.
Bye low, bye, baby bye,
Angels guard thee in sleep.

BEDTIME PRAYER

Gentle Jesus, meek and mild,
Look upon a little child;
Pity my simplicity,
Suffer me to come to Thee.

Lamb of God, I look to Thee:
Thou shalt my example be;
Thou art gentle, meek and mild;
Thou wast once a little child.

Fain I would be as Thou art;
Give me Thy obedient heart.
Thou art pitiful and kind,
Let me have Thy loving mind.

Loving Jesus, gentle Lamb,
In Thy gracious hands I am:
Make me, Saviour, what Thou art;
Live Thyself within my heart.

CHARLES WESLEY

The embers of the day are red
Beyond the murky hill.
The kitchen smokes; the bed
In the darkling house is spread:
The great sky darkens overhead,
And the great woods are shrill.
So far have I been led,
Lord, by Thy will:
So far I have followed, Lord, and wondered
    still.
The breeze from the embalmed land
Blows sudden towards the shore,
And claps my cottage door.
I hear the signal, Lord—I understand.
The night at Thy command
Comes. I will eat and sleep and will not
    question more.

ROBERT LOUIS STEVENSON

In Praise of Little Children

CHILDHOOD

Childhood is cutting the top off a hill to let the sun shine through.

Childhood is digging a hole to China to see who's there.

Childhood is measles, whooping cough, bellyache and glorious days home from school to recuperate.

Childhood is finding a bird's egg, catching a baby rabbit, cuddling a kitten, hooking a fish, being chased by a bull, being barked at by a dog, and having the horse you're trying to catch run away from you again and again and again.

Childhood is knowing Mother or Dad will be there when you get home and knowing someone who loves you will take you on your favorite excursion.

Children never stay the same, never stand still, never know when they've had enough ice cream, loving or green apples.

From LAUS INFANTIUM

In praise of little children I will say
God first made man, then found a better
    way
For woman, but his third way was the best.
Of all created things the loveliest
And most divine are children. Nothing here
Can be to us more gracious or more dear.
And though when God saw all his works
    were good
There was no rosy flower of babyhood,
'Twas said of children in a later day
That none could enter Heaven save such as
    they.

WILLIAM CANTON

A boy is nature's answer to that false belief that there is no such thing as perpetual motion. A boy can swim like a fish, run like a deer, climb like a squirrel, balk like a mule, bellow like a bull, eat like a pig, or act like a jackass, according to climatic conditions. He is a piece of skin stretched over an appetite; a noise covered with smudges. He is a growing animal of superlative promise, to be fed, watered, and kept warm, a joy forever, a periodic nuisance, the problem of our times, the hope of a nation. Every boy is evidence that God is not yet discouraged of man.

TO BE A GIRL

To be a girl, and see
Beauty in flower, bird and tree;
To follow truth and right, and know
The emptiness of outward show.

To be a girl, and thrill
When climbing windblown up the hill;
To think the Father's love and care
Are round about, and everywhere.

To be a girl, and aim
Above the mark of self and fame;
To pass through, strong, and pure, and
    good,
The gate which leads to womanhood.

To be a girl, and heed
The call to meet the world's great need
Put Beauty, Truth and Goodness first,
Bring in the Kingdom of our God.

Building boys is better than mending men.

CHARLES H. SPURGEON

I never meet a ragged boy on the street
without feeling that I owe him a salute, for
I know not what possibilities may be but-
toned up under that shabby coat.

JAMES A. GARFIELD

From BOY OR GIRL?

Some folks pray for a boy, and some
  For a golden-haired girl to come.
Some claim to think there is more joy
  Wrapped up in the smile of a little boy,
While others pretend that the silky curls
  And plump pink cheeks of the little girls
Bring more of bliss to the old home place,
  Than a small boy's queer little freckled
    face.

Now which is better, I couldn't say
  If the Lord should ask me to choose
    today;
If He should put in a call for me
  And say: "Now what shall your order be,
A boy or girl? I have both in store—
  Which of the two are you waiting for?"
I'd say with one of my broadest grins:
  "Send either one, if it can't be twins."

EDGAR A. GUEST

Know you what it is to be a child? It is to be
something very different from the man of
today. It is to have a spirit yet streaming
from the waters of baptism; it is to believe
in love, to believe in loveliness, to believe in
belief.

FRANCIS THOMPSON

GIRLS' NAMES

What lovely names for girls there are!
There's Stella like the Evening Star,
And Sylvia like a rustling tree,
And Lola like a melody,
And Flora like a flowery morn,
And Sheila like a field of corn,
And Melusina like the moan
Of water. And there's Joan, like Joan.

ELEANOR FARJEON

BOYS' NAMES

What splendid names for boys there are!
There's Carol like a rolling car,
And Martin like a flying bird,
And Adam like the Lord's First Word,
And Raymond like the harvest Moon,
And Peter like a piper's tune,
And Alan like the flowing on
Of water. And there's John, like John.

ELEANOR FARJEON

MIRACLE

How could this lump of protoplasm,
Strictly Tomboy gender . . .
Suddenly be transformed into
A thing so sweet and tender?

How could we possibly have seen
The miracle take place,
When it worked stealthily behind
A freckled, dirty face?

GLADYS WHITNEY

Little children are the symbol of the eternal
marriage between love and duty.

GEORGE ELIOT

I hope we never run out of little girls. It does every heart good to see them dressed up in the spring of the year. When one bunch of little girls grow up, they promptly and beneficently produce another crop of little girls. Between the ages of 3 and 8 the little girl is the best example of the human race.

HARRY GOLDEN

THE RIGHTS OF A CHILD

The right to affection, love, and understanding.

The right to adequate nutrition and medical care.

The right to free education.

The right to full opportunity for play and recreation.

The right to a name and nationality.

The right to special care, if handicapped.

The right to be among the first to receive relief in times of disaster.

The right to learn to be a useful member of society and to develop individual abilities.

The right to be brought up in a spirit of peace and universal brotherhood.

The right to enjoy these rights, regardless of race, color, sex, religion, national or social origin.

UNITED NATIONS

A happy childhood is one of the best gifts that parents have it in their power to bestow.

MARY CHOLMONDELEY

The older I grow, the more I appreciate children. Children are the most wholesome part of the race, the sweetest, for they are freshest from the hand of God. Whimsical, ingenious, mischievous, they fill the world with joy and good humor. We adults live a life of apprehension as to what they will think of us; a life of defense against their terrifying energy; a life of hard work to live up to their great expectations. We put them to bed with a sense of relief—and greet them in the morning with delight and anticipation. We envy them the freshness of adventure and the discovery of life. In all these ways, children add to the wonder of being alive. In all these ways, they help to keep us young.

HERBERT HOOVER

Once you've loved a child, you love all children. You give away your love to one, and you find that by the giving you have made yourself an inexhaustible treasury.

MARGARET LEE RUNBECK

TO A GRANDDAUGHTER

Jennifer has golden hair,
Cornflower-blue blue eyes.
She's just as big as half a pint—
A most enchanting size!

For all she is so tiny
Her strength's beyond compare.
She wraps me 'round her finger
And keeps me helpless there!

VIVIAN C. ISGRIG

A LITTLE GIRL

A little girl is a skipping rope
Tilting and turning around,
A little girl has stars in her eyes
Though her feet are on the ground;
A little girl is a ballet dress,
And pointed, outstretched toes,
A little girl is a lullaby
For a babe in dolly clothes.
A little girl has eyes aglow
With love for dad and mother,
And her knight in shining armor is
Her two-year-older brother.

KAY WISSINGER

TODAY

Many things can wait—the child cannot.
Right now his hip bones are being formed,
his blood is being made, his senses are
being developed. To him or her we cannot
say tomorrow. His or her name is today.

GABRIELA MISTRAL

From ODE ON INTIMATIONS OF IMMORTALITY

Our birth is but a sleep and a forgetting;
The Soul that rises with us, our Life's Star,
    Hath had elsewhere its setting
    And cometh from afar;
    Nor in entire forgetfulness,
    And not in utter nakedness,
But trailing clouds of glory do we come
    From God, who is our home:
Heaven lies about us in our infancy!

WILLIAM WORDSWORTH

Children get us down on the floor, up on the latest commercials, out of change, 'way out searching for the ultimate philosophic truths.

Children make some of our nightmares come true and many of our dreams too—the good ones.

ALEC J. LANGFORD

BILL OF RIGHTS

A boy has a right to the pursuit of happiness. He has the right to the kind of play that will stretch his imagination, tax his ingenuity, sharpen his wits, challenge his prowess, and keep his self-starter going.

He has the right to the satisfaction of that thirst to explore the world around him, every bit of which is new to him, and to explore the land of make-believe at will.

He has the right to affection and friendship. He has the right to the sense of security in belonging to some group. He is by nature gregarious, and the cultivation of that instinct will bring him many joys and helps in life.

He has the right to health protections that will make him an inch taller than his dad. He has the right to education and training that will fit him into a job he likes when he becomes a man.

HERBERT HOOVER

The childhood shows the man as morning shows the day.

JOHN MILTON

PRAYER

Oh, God, make me a better parent. Help me to understand my children, to listen patiently to what they have to say and to understand all their questions kindly. Keep me from interrupting them, talking back to them and contradicting them. Make me as courteous to them as I would have them be to me. Give me the courage to confess my sins against my children and ask them forgiveness, when I know that I have done wrong.

May I not vainly hurt the feelings of my children. Forbid that I should laugh at their mistakes, or resort to shame and ridicule as punishment. Let me not tempt a child to lie and steal. So guide me hour by hour that I may demonstrate by all I say and do that honesty produces happiness.

Reduce, I pray, the meanness in me. May I cease to nag; and when I am out of sorts, help me, O Lord, to hold my tongue. Blind me to the little errors of my children and help me to see the good things that they do. Give me a ready word for honest praise.

Help me to treat my children as those of their own age, but let me not exact of them the judgments and conventions of adults. Allow me not to rob them of the opportunity to wait upon themselves, to think, to choose, and to make their own decisions.

Forbid that I should ever punish them for my selfish satisfaction. May I grant them all their wishes that are reasonable and have the courage always to withhold a privilege which I know will do them harm.

Make me so fair and just, so considerate and companionable to my children that they will have genuine esteem for me. Fit me to be loved and imitated by my children. Oh, God, do give me calm and poise and self-control.

GARRY C. MYERS

HANDS

A child is two wee hands always eager to help at the wrong time. Hands clumsy enough to spill glasses of milk continually and to drop cookie crumbs on the clean carpet. Yet hands gentle enough and caring enough to bandage a puppy's sore paw. A child is a pair of kind hands directly connected to a warm heart whenever there is a stray cat in the neighborhood.

MARKY WILLIS SCHMIDT

Each child carries his own blessing into the world.

YIDDISH PROVERB

Children of all ages have one thing in common—they close their ears to advice and open their eyes to example.

ROBERT HAAS

Children need love, especially when they don't deserve it.

HAROLD S. HULBERT

TO MY CHILD

You are the trip I did not take;
You are the pearls I cannot buy;
You are my blue Italian lake;
You are my piece of foreign sky.

ANNE CAMPBELL

CLOUD DREAMS

I saw two little children
Dreaming in the sun,
With that far-away make believe look in
    their eyes
That makes dreams and reality—one.

Said one little dreamer, "Let's just pretend
That I live on that cloud up there!
But you're an animal here below—
A horse—or a dog—or a bear!
And while you run and work and play
—I'll just lay!"

Her partner in dreams looked wistfully
At the fluffy white cloud in the sky,
Accepting her dull prosaic role
With a heavy earth-bound sigh.
Then suddenly she cried with glee
"I'll be a horse with *wings*," said she,
"And while you lie—I'll just fly!"

GLADYS WHITNEY

Sometimes looking deep into the eyes of a child, you are conscious of meeting a glance full of wisdom. The child has known nothing yet but love and beauty. All this piled-up world knowledge you have acquired is unguessed at by him. And yet you meet this wonderful look that tells you in a moment more than all the years of experience have seemed to teach.

HILDEGARDE HAWTHORNE

Our Family Grows

_____ was born on _____

at _____

_____ was born on _____

at _____

_____ was born on _____

at _____

_____ was born on _____

at _____

_____ was born on _____

at _____

Photographs

Photographs

School Days

The job of a teacher is to excite in the young a boundless sense of curiosity about life, so that the growing child shall come to apprehend it with an excitement tempered by awe and wonder.

JOHN GARRETT

PRAYER AT A PLACE OF LEARNING

O God, most graciously thou walkest here,
Thy footsteps echoing. These are thy halls
Of learning, these the colonnaded walls
That know thy revelation firm and clear.
All zeal and purpose come from thee,
   O Lord.
The cultivated mind, the healing hand
Are yet thine instruments. Give to this land
Thy music, handiwork, and holy word.
Grant that the universe may know thy face,
Thy measured music heard from every
   tower,
Thy handiwork revealed in every hour,
That every child and man may learn thy
   grace.
O God, who walkest here in gardens bright,
Guide us forever to reveal thy light.

KENNETH HEAFIELD

The art of teaching is the art of assisting discovery.

MARK VAN DOREN

TASK

To build up in every man and woman a solid core of spiritual life, which will resist the attrition of everyday existence in our mechanized world—that is the most difficult and important task of school and university.

RICHARD LIVINGSTONE

FIRST DAY IN SCHOOL

The little fellow trooped down the road
   As excited as could be,
Down to the corner to catch the bus,
   With a kiss and a wave went he.

And all my heart went with him,
   As I smiled to see him go,
For on! it's a whole new world he'll find,
   And its pitfalls are many, I know.

May the angels of every boy's Father
   Guard him all his life's way,
Keep his conscience true and tender,
   From this his first school day!

ALMETA HILTY GOOD

FIRST DAY OF TEACHING

Now this is new: that I (habitué
Of classes where my thinking has been
   stirred
To surging tide or frothy ripple) stand
Before a class to speak instructive word.
I planned to have it so. Deliberately
I laid foundation for this moment. Yet . . .
I did not know my feet would feel so
   large . . .
O God of Teachers, may I not forget
Those neat assignments, practiced to the
   letter,
Those deftly fashioned phrases that I
   planned.
Now must I pass these papers. O dear God,
Let not the sheets go slithering from my
   hand.
And if You could but ring the fire alarm . . .
Or anything . . . O any sharp surprise
To turn away from my stiff dwindling self
These thirty pair of adolescent eyes.

BONARO W. OVERSTREET

LETTER TO THE WORLD

World, take my son by the hand. My son starts to school tomorrow. It's all going to be strange and new to him for awhile, and I wish you would sort of treat him gently.

You see, up to now, he's been the king of the roost. He's been boss of the backyard. I have always been around to repair his wounds and I've always been handy to soothe his feelings.

But now things are going to be different.

This morning he's going to walk down the front steps, wave his hand and start his great adventure. It's an adventure that will probably include wars and tragedy and sorrow. To live his life in the world he has to live in will require faith and love and courage.

So, world, I wish you would sort of take him by his young hand and teach him the things he will have to know. Teach him— but gently, if you can.

He will have to learn, I know, that all men are not just, that all men are not true. Teach him that for every scoundrel there is a hero, that for every crooked politician there is a dedicated leader. Teach him that for every enemy there is a friend.

Let him learn early that the bullies are the easiest people to lick.

Teach him the wonders of books. Give him quiet time to ponder the eternal mystery of birds in the sky, bees in the sun, and flowers on a green hill.

Teach him it is far more honorable to fail than to cheat. Teach him to have faith in his own ideas, even if everyone tells him they are wrong.

Try to give my son the strength not to follow the crowd when everyone else is getting on the bandwagon. Teach him to listen to all men—but to filter all he hears on a screen of truth and to take only the good that comes through.

Teach him to sell his brawn and brains to the highest bidder, but never to put a price tag on his heart and soul.

Teach him to close his ears to a howling mob—and to stand and fight if he thinks he's right.

Teach him gently, world, but don't coddle him, because only the test of fire makes fine steel.

This is a big order, world, but see what you can do.

Christians believe education should never end. Do not use your diplomas as a padlock on your mind. Do not regard graduation from any educational institution as graduation from the task of getting an education. Responsibility for nurture and growth of the mind is a life-long assignment to every human being by the Author of wisdom.

EVERETT W. PALMER

Seventh graders come in assorted sizes, weights, and colors. They may be either boys or girls and will likely be found scuffling with, shouting at, running to, or whispering about. Their pockets and purses bulge with puzzles, bits of plastic, bean shooters, bedraggled lipsticks, pictures, and rubber bands—but no pencils.

HELEN P. CHAPMAN

A child's education should begin at least one hundred years before he was born.

OLIVER WENDELL HOLMES

TWO TEMPLES

A Builder builded a temple,
  He wrought it with grace and skill;
Pillars and groins and arches,
  All fashioned to work his will.
Men said, as they saw its beauty,
  "It shall never know decay;
Great is thy skill, O Builder!
  Thy fame shall endure for aye."

A Teacher builded a temple
  With loving and infinite care,
Planning each arch with patience,
  Laying each stone with prayer.
None praised her unceasing efforts,
  None knew of her wondrous plan,
For the temple the Teacher builded
  Was unseen by the eyes of man.

Gone is the Builder's temple,
  Crumbled into the dust;
Low lies each stately pillar,
  Food for consuming rust.
But the temple the Teacher builded
  Will last while the ages roll,
For that beautiful unseen temple
  Was child's immortal soul.

HATTIE VOSE HALL

Your diploma is your ticket to the adventure of life. It's your certificate saying that schooldays are past and that now you are qualified and ready for whatever the future holds. What a thrill to leave the known for the unknown, to push off into the mystery of excitement of tomorrow. Yours is the challenge to go places and do things and become someone in the thriving world. Congratulations and God go with you all the way.

NORMAN VINCENT PEALE

THE UNIVERSITY

There are few earthly things more beautiful than a university. It is a place where those who hate ignorance may strive to know, where those who perceive truth may strive to make others see; where seekers and learners alike, banded together in the search for knowledge, will honour thought in all its finer ways, will welcome thinkers in distress or in exile, will uphold ever the dignity of thought and learning and will exact standards in these things. They give to the young their impressionable years, the bond of a lofty purpose shared, of a great corporate life whose links will not be loosed until they die. They give young people that close companionship for which youth longs, and that chance of the endless discussion of the themes which are endless, without which youth would seem a waste of time.

JOHN MASEFIELD

The purpose of the classroom is not to inform but to transform.

PATRICIA RISDON

ON THE ADDING OF "UNDER GOD" TO THE PLEDGE OF ALLEGIANCE

From this day forward the millions of our school children will daily proclaim in city and town, every village and rural schoolhouse, the dedication of our nation and our people to the Almighty. To anyone who truly loves America nothing could be more inspiring than to contemplate this rededication of our youth on each school morning to our country's true meaning.

DWIGHT D. EISENHOWER

THE STUDENT CREED

I pledge to develop a deeper appreciation
of myself, my country, and my Creator.

I believe in myself. I must have the
confidence to pursue successfully my
vocation and to attain my goal in life.

I believe in my school. It provides an
opportunity to acquire the skills of
my vocation, the knowledge to earn
my living, and the culture to
teach me how to live.

I believe in my country. America has
made available to man the world's
greatest bulwark of freedom. I
pledge to keep it so.

I believe in a Supreme Being. Life's
gifts and privileges are ultimately
derived from God. Without faith I
will perish.

I pledge to uphold these ideals. I
will respect myself and obey the
regulations of my school, the laws
of my country, and the commandments
of my Creator.

TO A DAUGHTER, GRADUATING

What shall you carry
along to tomorrow?
Put in your pocket
a smile but no sorrow.
Take in your heart
the green fields of the spring,
the width of the sky,
the joy of a swing.
Keep in your spirit
the sunlight of sharing,
the feeling of worth,
the answer of caring.

VIRGINIA COVEY BOSWELL

PRAYER FOR TEACHERS

Lord, it helps me to remember that You
were a teacher. You were a lot of other
things, but there is something very human
and reassuring in Your giving the word of
life to restless, uncertain people. You never
used a chalkboard, corrected exams, or sat
through a graduation ceremony. But You
rejoiced with men and women and little
children who discovered for the first time
what it means to be sons and daughters of a
good Father. Grant a full measure of Your
spirit to those whose task it is to awaken
minds and hearts to the wonders of creation, the insights of science, the relation of
cause and effect. They often get discouraged, Lord. Lift them up by Your example
and power.

THE CHRISTOPHERS

LIBERAL EDUCATION

That man, I think, has had a liberal education who has been so trained in youth that
his body is the ready servant of his will and
does with ease and pleasure all the work, as
a mechanism, it is capable of; whose intellect is a clear, cold-logic engine, with all its
parts of equal strength, and in smooth
working order; ready, like a steam engine,
to be turned to any kind of work, and spin
the gossamers as well as forge the anchors
of the mind; whose mind is stored with a
knowledge of the great laws of its operations; one who is no stunted ascetic, is full
of life and fire, but whose passions are
trained to come to heel by a vigorous will,
the servant of a tender conscience; who has
learned to love all beauty, whether of
nature or of art; to hate all vileness; and to
respect others as himself.

THOMAS HUXLEY

COMMENCEMENT PRAYER

O Lord, as we leave this University today and take fleeting glances backward, we are painfully aware of unopened books, of valuable classes that we cut, of opportunities that we wasted, of times when our effort was poor. We confess our sins and ask in repentance for pardon. We are thankful for blessings which were unpleasant—a deservedly poor grade, a merited rejection, a rebuff. These taught us decency and discipline.

We thank Thee for the professor who really cared, for the teacher who opened new windows in our minds, the one who gave us wisdom as well as facts. We are grateful for the student who accepted us for what we were, who listened when we poured out our troubles, who encouraged us to believe in our possibilities. We thank Thee for fellow students who were righteous without being rude, who were able to see the difference between improving a university and destroying it.

As we go from this place, we pray Thee to keep us from captivity to ideas that have lost their force, but help us to remember the lessons of history we have learned here so that we may not be doomed to repeat the mistakes of history. As we go out into the world, show us how to be responsibly involved in its creative improvement. Help us to find the right mixture of a serious mind and a light heart. May each of us have the scholar's approach and everyone remain teachable. We pray in the name of the great Teacher of Nazareth.

HOWARD C. WILKINSON

Lord, speak to me, that I may speak
  In living echoes of Thy tone;
As Thou hast sought, so let me seek
  Thy erring children lost and lone.

O teach me, Lord, that I may teach
  The precious things Thou dost impart;
And wing my words, that they may reach
  The hidden depths of many a heart.

O fill me with Thy fullness, Lord,
  Until my very heart o'erflow
In kindling thought and glowing word,
  Thy love to tell, Thy praise to show.

O use me, Lord, use even me,
  Just as Thou wilt, and when and where;
Until They blessed face I see,
  Thy rest, Thy joy, Thy glory share.

FRANCES HAVERGAL

PRAYER OF A BEGINNING TEACHER

Dear God, I humbly pray
  That Thou, with each passing day
  Wilt give me courage, wisdom true,
To meet each problem, see it thru—
  With wisdom and justice to teach each
    child
  To recognize the things worthwhile.
Help me to start them on the way
  To clean, brave living—day by day,
  So that tomorrow for each one
  Will be met squarely—and be won—
And as I help each little child
  To learn to love the things worthwhile,
  Lord, help me to be true;
  For I am just beginning, too.

OUIDA SMITH DUNNAM

SCULPTING

I took a piece of plastic clay
And idly fashioned it one day.
And as my fingers pressed it still
It moved and yielded to my will.

I came again when days were past:
The bit of clay was hard at last.
The form I gave it still it bore,
And I could fashion it no more!

I took a piece of living clay,
And gently pressed it day by day,
And moulded with my power and art
A young child's soft and yielding heart.

I came again when years had gone:
It was a man I looked upon.
He still that early impress bore,
And I could fashion it no more!

WHAT IS EDUCATION?

Knowledge does not comprise all which is
in the term education. The feelings are to be
disciplined, passions to be restrained, true
and worthy motives to be inspired, a profound religious feeling to be instilled, and
pure morality inculcated under all circumstances. All this is comprised in education.

DANIEL WEBSTER

True education combines intellect, beauty,
goodness, and the greatest of these is goodness. When we do the best that we can, we
never know what miracle is wrought in our
life, or in the life of another.

HELEN KELLER

TO THE GRADUATE

You are the cornerstone on which
 we build
Our highest hopes. Today, our
 hearts are filled
With joy because you've reached
 the cherished goal
You struggled for with all your
 heart and soul.
Stride out, your flag of shining
 dreams unfurled;
Today, a doorway opens on the
 world!

LOUISE HAJEK

GRADUATION

In caps and gowns they seem the same,
Sedately marching two by two;
I wait to hear a special name—
And then my child comes into view!

My daughter, through another's eyes,
May bear resemblance to the rest;
But through this doting mother's eyes,
She is the sweetest—and the best.

NOVA TRIMBLE ASHLEY

Reading should be for children an integral
part of life, like eating and loving and
playing. An early familiarity with books
unconsciously introduces the child to the
fundamental, liberating truth: that the
largest part of the universe of space and
time can never be apprehended by direct
firsthand experience.

CLIFTON FADIMAN

Family Autographs

Photographs

The Bloom of Youth

From MORITURI SALUTAMUS

How beautiful is youth! how bright it
    gleams
With its illusions, aspirations, dreams!
Book of Beginnings, Story without End,
Each maid a heroine, and each man a
    friend!

           HENRY WADSWORTH LONGFELLOW

Those who can pray and sing and tell old
tales have found the secret of perpetual
youth.

           GEORGE A. BUTTRICK

OREMUS

This is my daughter,
Picture superimposed on picture,
The edges blurring, but I know them well,
I can decipher them.
First, chubby-legged, her bonnet made of
    organdy,
She merges into plaid and braids
And ink-stained books;
And etched on top of that there is a Brownie
    uniform.
I trace her figure, sturdy, brave,
Perched upon her pony.
How changed, with lipstick now,
And hopes to match her bright blue eyes,
She rustles in her party dress.
I let her go tonight,
I trusted her to gasoline and steel
And to the fragile judgment of
A boy just lately from a chrysalis
Of jeans and frogs and Little League.
And all my thoughts whirl in a centrifuge—
God keep her safe for me.

           RUTH STAUNTON

SALUTE TO YOUTH

You are the hope of the world.
You are radiant with energy.
You are undaunted by impossibilities.
You believe in the basic honesty of men.
You face life as a Great Adventure.
You dream noble dreams.
Your marching feet beat a symphony of
    progress!

Of you we expect great things:
The conquest of disease;
The outlawing of war;
The dawn of the more abundant life;
The harmonizing of industry;
The creation of beauty;
The revival of the spirit!

As you march into the future with banners
    flying,
Eyes shining with the splendor of your
    ideals,
We doff our hats and stand at salute.
For you are the hope of the world!

           WILFERD A. PETERSON

A TEENAGE SON

He grasps a wrench in each his hands,
as in the dirty shop he stands.
He cleans, adjusts, and overhauls—
a greasy king in coveralls.

           MRS. CARL LUNDGREN

A child educated only at school is an un-
educated child.

           GEORGE SANTAYANA

TO MY DAUGHTER

There are so many things I try to say
While you half listen, lost in your own
    dreams.
I want to point out pitfalls, smooth your
    way,
For love is not all roses and moonbeams.
But who am I to caution or advise?
Just Mother, who has never known the joy
Of love like yours—a kiss, eyes meeting
    eyes,
And all the bright world centered in one
    boy!

Yet as I sigh, I suddenly recall
My mother's sighs—how many years ago!
And see the young are all alike, and all
Must find out for themselves that they may
    grow.
And middle age grows too. I'm just
    discerning
That half the joy of love is in the learning.

VIRGINIA SHEARER HOPPER

A youth is a person who is going to carry on
what you have started. He is going to sit
where you are sitting and, when you are
gone, attend to those things which you
think are important. You may adopt all the
policies you please, but how they will be
carried out depends on him. He will assume
control of your duties, states, and nation.
He is going to move in and take over your
churches, schools, universities, and cor-
porations. All your books are going to be
judged, praised, or condemned by him. The
fate of humanity is in his hands.

OHIO MASON

Albert Schweitzer, when asked three essen-
tials for the bringing up of a child, replied,
"Example, example, example."

HE WAS MY TEACHER

He harrowed minds with curving question
    marks,
Teaching as much outside the book as in;
He'd listen out the window for Spring larks,
Postponing Euclid's chalky discipline.

He kept the burr of "Why?" beneath the tail
Of every sluggard slouched down in his
    seat,
Our spines came straight—we did not dare
    to fail,
And we survived by thinking on our feet.

He was my teacher—wise—yet hard as
    knots,
I tried to pick him loose and so undo him.
But he was miles ahead of all my plots;
I've found instead that he has tied me to
    him.

RALPH W. SEAGER

SEEKING

The young will always seek life. Let them
find us among the living. Then we can share
life together.

ROBERT J. MUELLER

SCOUTING

Scouting is a boy looking up to a man and wishing in his heart that he could be more like that man, and the man admiring the boy and wishing he were more like him.

Scouting is a group of boys sitting around a campfire in silence. No words are spoken, but the group is being welded into a team.

Scouting is a group of boys pulling together with a group of men for the common good. It is men doing things with rather than for boys.

Scouting is mother sewing on merit badges and an entire family proud of each advancement.

Scouting is noise and action and food and fun. It is play and release from restraint, yet it is purposeful and resultful.

Scouting is a boy setting his own goals and pushing himself toward their accomplishment. It is a man rating high what a boy is reaching for.

Scouting is the President of the United States—and the newest eight-year-old Cub Scout.

It is the youth of America today in earnest about America's tomorrow.

WALTER MacPEEK

Whatever God calls us to do He also makes possible for us to accomplish.

Youth, what man's age is like to be doth
    show,
We may our ends by our beginnings know.

JOHN DENHAM

From THE BAREFOOT BOY

Blessings on thee, little man,
Barefoot boy, with cheek of tan!
With thy turned-up pantaloons,
And thy merry whistled tunes;
With thy red lip, redder still
Kissed by strawberries on the hill;
With the sunshine on thy face,
Through thy torn brim's jaunty grace;
From my heart I give thee joy,—
I was once a barefoot boy!

JOHN GREENLEAF WHITTIER

FATHER'S LEGACY

You thought you failed because you could
    not give
The many things you wished to ease my
    way;
But you did more; you taught me how to
    live,
And filled with priceless thoughts each
    passing day.
You made me find in every book a friend
And made me see a story in each face.
You pointed to the heights, and yet could
    bend
To search for God beneath the common-
    place.
I wonder if you know how rich I feel,
How much I prize this legacy from you;
You called yourself a failure, yet I kneel
And pray that, in your way, I may fail, too.

EUGENE FAIN

TO A YOUNG GIRL

Your laughter is a fount of radiance
Which thrills the vivid air as you lilt by;
Your feet are sandaled like the April wind's,
That lovely wayward daughter of the sky.

Your brow is bright with dreams, your lips
        upcurved
With sweetness of your thought; in your
        clear eyes
That still hold shining wonder in their
        deeps
The unspent glory of the morning lies.

HESTER SUTHERS

Children tend to adopt the beliefs of those whom they instinctively recognize as happy.

WILLIAM ERNEST HOCKING

Through our great good fortune, in our youth our hearts were touched with fire. It was given us to learn at the outset that life is a profound and passionate thing.

OLIVER WENDELL HOLMES

Interest in the changing seasons is a much happier state of mind than being hopelessly in love with spring.

GEORGE SANTAYANA

FAMILIAR STRANGER

Mother looked up at her oldest son,
Now come of age with twenty-one

Birthdays filling him out to size,
But sons stay small in a mother's eyes.

Then she gazed downward through the
        years,
The months of joy, the days of tears;

The marks on the door that told how tall,
The cowboy wallpaper on the wall;

That day she felt her hair turn grey
when he and Rover ran away;

But both were there for bed-time prayer,
And the gold came back into her hair.

Remembering his slam-bang "See you,
        Mom!"
As she straightened his tie for the Junior
        Prom.

She raised her eyes again to scan
Her son, and saw a strange, new man.

RALPH W. SEAGER

A high school girl has the energy of a miniature atomic bomb, the lungs of an auctioneer, the curiosity of a cat, the imagination of Edgar A. Poe, the fault-finding ability of a bookkeeper, the irresponsibility of a butterfly, and the friendliness of a bus driver.

JOYCE BASS

Growing Pains

True worth is in being, not seeming;
    In doing each day that goes by
Some little good—not in the dreaming
    Of great things to do by-and-by.
For whatever men say in blindness,
    And spite of the fancies of youth,
There's nothing so kingly as kindness,
    And nothing so royal as truth.

We get back our mete as we measure;
    We cannot do wrong and feel right;
Nor can we give pain and gain pleasure,
    For justice avenges each slight.
The air for the wing of the sparrow,
    The bush for the robin and wren,
But always the path that is narrow
    And straight for the children of men.

ALICE CARY

Ideals and principles continue from generation to generation only when they are built into the hearts of children as they grow up.

GEORGE S. BENSON

A child is always becoming and never standing still.

MAJA BERNATH

To a little child, security lies in the familiar: the well-known voice or face, food or plaything. Later security is found in the well-known locality and playmate. But most of all, the child needs the assurance of parental love, the knowledge that no matter what he might do, his parents will always love him even though they may not love what he does. It is well for a child to learn he is responsible for his actions, but also that his parents are always at his side. Even a little child can learn that if he kicks over the wastebasket in a temper tantrum he will have to pick up the mess. But his mother may show her love by helping him.

PHILIP M. STIMSON

MOTHER LOVE

The eagle builds a hard and hostile nest
To house her fledglings, lining it with
        stones
And sticks and thorns. Her little, stirring
        ones
Do not know cradled comfort, downy rest—
But all about, the breath of heaven sings;
The lifting mountains beckon to the
        heights;
The sun allures them, and the sky invites,
And soon the feathered eaglets find their
        wings!
She knows the way that eagle wings
        must go,
That only from untender nurturing
In rugged nests do strong young eagles
        spring—
She will not let them rest content below
When it is time for winged ones to rise,
No mother-softness robs them of their
        skies!

ROSELLE MERCIER MONTGOMERY

THE FAMILY STAIRS

There in the upper hallway
New stairs lift and climb
Closer to the starlight
And built of passing time.

Each stair tread is a marking
Levelled to fine-spun hair,
And each is signed by the owner
When his head was there.

The pencil marks go upward,
And every level can
Declare so much the nearer
To woman or to man.

The mother and the father
Work and fetch and call
And may not see the poem
Growing on their wall.

They look over years around them
To years that are to be
When happiness they live in
Will cool to history.

And one day all the marks there
Level out for good,
And there is only silence
Where the children stood.

Down below the staircase
A man and woman sit
And think of the upstairs poem
And how they fashioned it.

ROBERT P. TRISTRAM COFFIN

Every word and deed of a parent is a fiber
woven into the character of a child, which
ultimately determines how that child fits
into the fabric of society.

DAVID WILKERSON

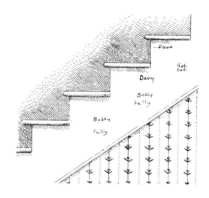

Lucky the lad whose teachers know
That it takes time for a boy to grow;
That Rome was not achieved in a day.
Nor a boy perfected the easy way;
Teachers view his falls from grace,
His strident voice, his reckless pace,
His scorn for dentrifice and soap
With an inexhaustible fund of hope.
Lucky the lad whose teachers know
That it takes time for a boy to grow.

MAY RICHSTONE

LOSING BATTLE

This, I have learned,
Is children's technique:
They whittle you down
Till you're helplessly weak.
Then even the smallest,
Most innocent tyke,
Instinctively knowing
The moment, will strike.
So here is the sequence,
No parent can win:
First you give out,
And then you give in.

RICHARD ARMOUR

FIRST GOODBYE

You stand beside this little man,
   This eager, grown-up six-year-old,
And recollect the in-between
   That hurried him to this threshold.

He coos, he gurgles, jabbers, talks;
   He rolls, he creeps, he crawls, then walks.
From kiddie car he graduates,
   To wagon, scooter, roller skates.

The rattle box falls by the way,
   The building blocks have had their day.
Crayons and cutouts take their place,
   And comprehension shapes his face.

So give him books, unclasp his hand;
   Your fears, not his, you must command.
Since tears would only stay his wings,
   You smile, and wave your apron strings.
              MADELEINE LAEUFER

FIFTEENTH-CENTURY PETITION

Lord Jesus Christ, our Lord most dear,
As thou wast once an infant here,
So give this child of thine, we pray,
Thy grace and blessing day by day.
Thy saving grace on him bestow
That he in thee may live and grow.

The person who determines your way of living and your chance of salvation is not the man who pays your wages, nor your president, nor your doctor or policeman, nor yet even your spouse, but the one who looks you in the face when you are young, calls you by your true name, and says, "Go forth!"

              AGNES DE MILLE

TO MOTHERS EVERYWHERE

If you can guide, not push your son along,
If you can guard, not smother, from the
     wrong,
If you can love, not idolize your child,
If you can teach obedience, tame the wild
Instinctive moods, the very heart of him,
If you can pray, to save his soul from sin,
If you regard his need for elbow room,
And can remember he's a man so soon . . .
If you can punish, and be just, as well,
If you can, too, your rising anger quell,
If you respect his personality,
Give him to God for immortality,
If you can praise, where praise is rightly
     due,
If you can promise, and be ever true,
If you can trust him when there is some
     doubt
And then can tell him when no one's about,
If you can help him through the tender
     years,
If you can share his secrets and his fears,
If all God's laws you train him to uphold,
Your child will not forget you when
     you're old.
            IVY FLORENCE PEARMAN

RECIPE FOR RAISING CHILDREN

1 cup Proverbs 22:6
2 tablespoons Proverbs 19:18
A dash of Proverbs 23:1–8
A pinch of Ephesians 6:4
½ cup of Titus 2:3–7
Mix all ingredients, add a pound of persis-
   tence, one cup of love, and stir until the
   right consistency.

MOTHERHOOD

Someday, my son, I hope you know
The joy of watching a small boy grow.
A boy whose laughter makes you warm,
Whose antics run quite true to form.
Whose pants have patches on the knees,
Who climbs the tallest of the trees.
A boy who shelters all stray cats,
Who harbors dogs, and disdains hats.
Whose arms steal round your neck at night,
Whose hands are seldom ever white.
Who gives keen purpose to your life,
Who compensates for each day's strife.
All this I wish so you may know
The joy I had in watching you grow.

EMILY CAREY ALLEMAN

TO A CHILD GROWING UP

Little one,
you belong to yourself and God,
you are not mine;
I am only the port
that looses you into the bay,
the tide that bears you out
on your own adventure.

I am your sealegs,
your swift tack astride the wind;
I teach the bare mechanics of your craft.

But one day,
in the furor of a squall
or in the awful silence of a calm,
you'll find I'm not beside you at the helm;
and, if I've done my job right,
you will not be alone.

KAREN LIVINGSTON RAAB

A CHILD'S QUESTION

Will there really be a morning?
Is there such a thing as day?
Could I see it from the mountains
If I were as tall as they?

Has it feet like water-lilies?
Has it feathers like a bird?
Does it come from famous countries
Of which I have never heard?

Oh, some scholar, Oh, some sailor,
Oh, some wise man from the skies,
Please to tell a little pilgrim
Where the place called morning lies?

EMILY DICKINSON

Tho' growing with scarce a showing,
Yet, please God, we are growing.
The twig teacheth
The moth preacheth
The plant vaunteth
The bird chanteth
God's mercy overflowing.
Merciful past man's knowing.
Please God, to keep us growing.

CHRISTINA ROSSETTI

To be allowed to guide the life of a child is to be given an incredible compliment. It means that we are trusted with the responsibility of forming characters which may have eternal significance. No sensitive person can face this relationship without a deep sense of unworthiness as well as of honest reverence.

ELTON TRUEBLOOD

In Times of Trouble

I sought Him in a great cathedral, dim
With age, where oft-repeated prayers arise,
But caught no glimpse of Him.
I sought Him then atop a lonely hill,
Like Moses once, but though I scanned the
 skies,
My search was fruitless still.
There was a little home where grief and
 care
Had bred but courage, love, and valiant
 will,
I sought Him and found Him there.

ANNE MARRIOTT

Sunshine is delicious, rain is refreshing, wind braces up, snow is exhilarating; there is really no such thing as bad weather, only different kinds of good weather.

JOHN RUSKIN

A PHYSICIAN'S PRAYER

Give to my eyes the power to see
the hidden source of ill.
Give to my hands the healing touch,
the throb of pain to still.
Grant that my ears be swift to hear
the cry of those in pain.
Give to my tongue the words that bring
comfort and strength again.

CARING

I know I cannot enter all you feel
Nor bear with you the burden of your pain.
I can but offer what my love does give:
The strength of caring . . .
This I do in quiet ways
That on your lonely path
You may not walk alone.

HOWARD THURMAN

FACING A NEW DAY

As I enter this new day, God himself goes with me. His love, his care, his guidance, his protection surround me. They surround me as the silent sunlight surrounds a tree. If I encounter a difficult task, I can trust God to give me, through the processes operating within my body, the physical strength I must have. If I encounter a hard problem, I can trust God to give me, through the operations of my mind, the wisdom I need. If I must endure hardship, endure it because there is no honorable way of escape from it, I can trust God to give me the strength, the patience, the inward quietness which my difficult situation demands. I need never be afraid. I need never feel confused, bewildered, inadequate. Whatever happens, God's love and care encompass me. Secure within them I can face life, and any situation which life may create, undismayed.

JAMES GORDON GILKEY

CIRCUMSTANCES

People are always blaming their circumstances for what they are. I don't believe in circumstances. The people who get on in this world are the people who get up and look for the circumstances they want, and if they can't find them, they make them.

GEORGE BERNARD SHAW

From THE ENDURING HEARTH

If song and laughter warm the place
And faith and love the table grace,
Who keep it so need have no fears.
The home will stand throughout the years.

EDGAR A. GUEST

SUNSHINE

After a heavy rain the clearing process is a gradual one. First the rain lessens, then stops; stretches of blue sky increase and finally the sun shines through and the last clouds roll away. Likewise the stormy experiences of life clear up gradually, and we become impatient because the wounds of the spirit heal slowly. Yet as surely as the sun shines again after the storm, so the clouds of life will disappear, and there will be sunshine in our hearts again.

SUNSHINE MAGAZINE

HOLDING TOGETHER

The sea rises, the light fails, lovers cling to each other, and children cling to us. The moment we cease to hold each other, the sea engulfs us and the light goes out.

JAMES BALDWIN

This day someone with a burden can be helped by a letter from me.

EVELYN MATHEWS

Life consists not simply in what heredity and environment do to us but in what we make out of what they do to us.

HARRY EMERSON FOSDICK

A family is a unit composed not only of children but of men, women, an occasional animal, and the common cold.

Now, Father, now, in Thy dear presence
kneeling,
Our spirits yearn to feel Thy kindling
love:
Now make us strong, we need Thy deep
revealing
Of trust and strength and calmness from
above.

SAMUEL JOHNSON

STRENGTHENING

For every hill I've had to climb,
For every stone that bruised my feet,
For all the blood and sweat and grime,
For blinding storms and burning heat,
My heart sings but a grateful song—
These were the things that made me
strong!

For all the heart aches and the tears,
For all the anguish and the pain,
For gloomy days and fruitless years,
And for the hopes that lived in vain,
I do give thanks, for now I know
These were the things that helped me grow!

'Tis not the softer things of life
Which stimulate man's will to strive;
But bleak adversity and strife
Do most to keep man's will alive.
O'er rose-strewn paths the weaklings creep,
But brave hearts dare to climb the steep.

Time for Play

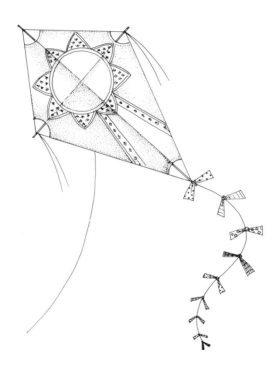

HUG O' WAR

I will not play at tug o' war.
I'd rather play at hug o' war,
Where everyone hugs
Instead of tugs,
Where everyone giggles
And rolls on the rug,
Where everyone kisses,
And everyone grins,
And everyone cuddles,
And everyone wins.

SHEL SILVERSTEIN

WORK AND PLAY

A great artist finds his play in his work. Play becomes art when raised to its highest excellence, its highest beauty, and its highest power. Anything that one does from cooking a dinner to governing a state becomes a work of art if motivated by the passion for excellence and done as well as it can be.

L. P. JACKS

No man is really depraved who can spend half an hour by himself on the floor playing with his little boy's electric train.

SIMEON STRUNSKY

MY KITE

Today I flew my long-tailed kite;
Up, up it went—'most out of sight.
I didn't have to do a thing
But tightly hold the ball of string.
I know what kept it up so high—
God's wind was blowing in the sky.

MARGUERITE LANE

THE TOY-STREWN HOME

Give me the house where the toys are
strewn,
  Where the dolls are asleep in the chairs,
Where the building blocks and the toy
balloon
  And the soldiers guard the stairs.
Let me step in the house where the tiny cart
  With the horses rules the floor,
And rest comes into my weary heart,
  For I am at home once more.

Give me the house with the toys about,
  With the battered old train of cars,
The box of paints and the books left out,
  And the ship with her broken spars.
Let me step in a house at the close of day
  That is littered with children's toys,
And dwell once more in the haunts of play,
  With the echoes of bygone noise.

Whoever has lived in a toy-strewn home,
  Though feeble he be and gray,
Will yearn, no matter how far he roam,
  For the glorious disarray
Of the little home with its littered floor
  That was his in the bygone days;
And his heart will throb as it throbbed
before,
  When he rests where a baby plays.

EDGAR A. GUEST

Couples should spend more time doing nothing.

JOHN R. FRY

WIN AND LOSE

Let others cheer the winning man,
There's one I hold worth while;
'Tis he who does the best he can,
Then loses with a smile.
Beaten he is, but not to stay
Down with the rank and file;
That man will win some other day,
Who loses with a smile.

From US TWO

Wherever I am, there's always Pooh,
There's always Pooh and Me.
Whatever I do, he wants to do,
"Where are you going to-day?" says Pooh:
"Well, that's very odd 'cos I was too.
"Let's go together," says Pooh, says he.
"Let's go together," says Pooh.

So wherever I am, there's always Pooh,
There's always Pooh and Me.
"What would I do?" I said to Pooh,
"If it wasn't for you," and Pooh said: "True,
It isn't much fun for One, but Two
Can stick together," says Pooh, says he.
"That's how it is," says Pooh.

A. A. MILNE

The real joy of life is in its play. Play is anything we do for the joy and love of doing it, apart from any profit, compulsion, or sense of duty. It is the real living of life with the feeling of freedom and self-expression. Play is the business of childhood, and its continuation in later years is the prolongation of youth.

WALTER RAUSCHENBUSCH

From OUR CIRCUS

We had a circus in our shed
(Admission, three new pins a head)
And every girl and boy I know
Is talking yet about our show.

They laughed so hard at Fatty Brown
When he came out to be the clown,
That all the neighbors ran to see
Whatever such a noise could be.

Our tin-pan and mouth-organ band
Played tunes that sounded simply grand;
We had a truly sawdust ring,
Pink lemonade, 'n everything.

The big menagerie was nice:
Three cats, one dog, and five white mice,
A parrot that Bill's uncle lent;
All underneath a bedspread tent.

LAURA LEE RANDALL

A man's real worth is determined by what he does when he has nothing to do.

MEGIDDO MESSAGE

Autographs of Special Friends

Photographs

Photographs

Furry Animals and
Other Friends

EVERY BOY SHOULD HAVE A DOG

Every boy should have a dog.
I've had it drummed into my ears
continually for seven years.
Of course, a boy should have a dog.

I have succumbed to pleading eye,
to smudge of mud on quivering chin,
his hopeful father joining in
to tell again the reasons why.

And now I find this muff of joy
that chews his shoes, that licks his face,
has proved beyond the slightest trace
that every dog should have a boy.

MYRA SCOVEL

THE SNOW-BIRD

When all the ground with snow is white,
    The merry snow-bird comes,
And hops about with great delight
    To find the scattered crumbs.

How glad he seems to get to eat
    A piece of cake or bread!
He wears no shoes upon his feet,
    Nor hat upon his head.

But happiest is he, I know,
    Because no cage with bars
Keeps him from walking on the snow
    And printing it with stars.

FRANK DEMPSTER SHERMAN

CATS

A black-nosed kitten will slumber all the
        day;
A white-nosed kitten is ever glad to play;
A yellow-nosed kitten will answer to your
        call;
And a gray-nosed kitten I like best of all.

A bird came down the walk,
He did not know I saw;
He bit an angleworm in halves
And ate the fellow, raw.

And then he drank a dew
From a convenient grass,
And then hopped sidewise to the wall
To let a beetle pass.

EMILY DICKINSON

GOD'S CREATURES

Hear our humble prayer, O God, for our friends the animals, thy creatures.

We pray especially for all that are suffering: for the overworked and underfed, the hunted, lost, or hungry; for all in captivity or ill-treated.

We entreat for them thy mercy and pity; and for those who deal with them we ask a heart of compassion, gentle hands, and kindly words.

Make us all to be true friends of animals, and so more worthy followers of our merciful Savior, Jesus Christ.

RODBOROUGH BEDE BOOK

To be popular at home is a great achievement. The man who is loved by the house cat, by the dog, by the neighbor's children, and by his own wife is a great man, even if he has never had his name in *Who's Who*.

THOMAS DREIER

WHAT ROBIN TOLD

How do robins build their nests?
  Robin Redbreast told me—
First a wisp of yellow hay
In a pretty round they lay;

Then some shreds of downy floss,
Feathers, too, and bits of moss,
Woven with a sweet, sweet song,
This way, that way, and across;
  That's what Robin told me.

Where do robins hide their nests?
  Robin Redbreast told me—
Up among the leaves so deep,
Where the sunbeams rarely creep,
Long before the winds are cold,
Long before the leaves are gold,
Bright-eyed stars will peep and see
Baby robins—one, two, three;
  That's what Robin told me.

GEORGE COOPER

MY DOG

His nose is short and scrubby;
  His ears hang rather low;
And he always brings the stick back,
  No matter how far you throw.

He gets spanked rather often
  For things he shouldn't do,
Like lying-on-beds, and barking,
  And eating up shoes when they're new.

He always wants to be going
  Where he isn't supposed to go.
He tracks up the house when it's snowing—
  Oh, puppy, I love you so.

MARCHETTE CHUTE

DEFEAT

I know the puppy's very new,
And I know that he's lonely too—
But puppy's place is in the shed,
And not with you, deep down in bed.
Tears will not move me—not at all,
Not even though he's soft and small,
And knows you when you come from play;
The shed's his place and there he'll stay,
    because—
Yes, he has lovely soft big paws,
And yes, I love his ears that flop....
Now, mind: not underneath! On top.

BARBARA A. JONES

May I love all thy creation, Lord. The whole
and every grain of sand of it. May I love
every leaf, every ray of thy light. May I love
the animals. Thou hast given them the rudi-
ments of thought and joy untroubled. Let
me not deprive them of their happiness. All
is like an ocean; all is flowing and blending.
To withhold a measure of love from anything in thy universe is to withhold the
same measure from Thee.

FEDOR DOSTOEVSKI

Backyard Magic

A GARDEN

A garden is a sunny room
Where peonies and pansies bloom,
A music hall where all day long
Birds fill the sheltered nooks with song.

A garden is a magic space
Where miracles are taking place,
And nature, out of leafy mold,
Produces phlox and marigold.

A garden is a gallery gay
With lovely pictures on display,
A church where stately lilies nod
And men draw very close to God.

EDGAR A. GUEST

Every child should have mudpies, grass-hoppers, waterbugs, tadpoles, frogs, mud turtles, elderberries, wild strawberries, acorns, chestnut trees to climb, brooks to wade in, water lilies, woodchucks, bats, bees, butterflies, various animals to pet, hayfields, pine cones, rocks to roll, sand, snakes, huckleberries and hornets; and any child who has been deprived of these has been deprived of the best part of his education.

LUTHER BURBANK

GOD'S HEART

The kiss of the sun for pardon,
  The song of the birds for mirth,
One is nearer God's heart in a garden
  Than anywhere else on earth.

PLANTING TIME

The earth's exuding life again;
The time has come to seize
Some moments for renewal
In the garden, on my knees.

My fingers mark the planting line
Through fragrant, fresh-turned sod;
My fingers seed and pat the soil,
And touch the hand of God.

IVA LILLGE

A LITTLE TREE

I never see a little tree bursting from the earth, peeping confidingly up among the withered leaves, without wondering how long it will live and what trials and triumphs it will have. It will better and beautify the earth; love the blue sky and the white clouds passing by and ever join merrily in the movement and the music of the elemental dance with the winds. It will welcome the flower-opening days of spring, be a home for the birds, and enjoy the quiet summer rain. And when comes the golden peace of autumn days I trust it will be ready with ripened fruit for the life to come. I never fail to hope that if this tree is cut down it may be used for a flag-pole to keep our glorious banner in the breeze, or be built into a cottage where love will abide, or if it must be burnt, that it will blaze on the hearthstone in a home where children play in the firelight on the floor.

ENOS A. MILLS

MIRACLE

Today I saw a miracle,
And when I looked around,
The world was full of miracles,
Just waiting to be found.

I saw a crocus burst in bloom,
Where once was barren earth;
I kissed a baby's cheek and knew
The miracle of birth.

I felt the velvet of a breeze,
I saw a sparrow fly.
I heard a sinner start to pray
Beneath a sunset sky.

Today I saw a miracle,
And when I looked around,
The world was full of miracles
Just waiting to be found.

JEAN FULLER RAUSCH

If a child is to keep alive his inborn sense of
wonder . . . he needs the companionship of
at least one adult who can share it, redis-
covering with him the joy, excitement, and
mystery of the world we live in.

RACHEL CARSON

There always will be gardens
For he who planted flowers
In Eden long and long ago,
Still takes a hand in ours.
And still he walks at eventide
In gardens cool and sweet.
The raptured roses touch his robe,
The violets kiss his feet.

LILIAN LEVERIDGE

From THE SINLESS CHILD

She early marked the butterfly,
   That gay, mysterious thing,
That, bursting from its prison-house
   Appeared on golden wing;
It had no voice to speak delight,
   Yet on the floweret's breast,
She saw it mute and motionless,
   In long, long rapture rest.

It crawled no more a sluggish thing
   Upon the lowly earth;
A brief, brief sleep, and then she saw
   A new and radiant birth,
And thus she learned without a doubt,
   That man from death would rise,
As did the butterfly on wings,
   To claim its native skies.

ELIZABETH OAKES SMITH

From THE PLANTING OF
THE APPLE TREE

What plant we in this apple tree?
Buds which the breath of summer days
Shall lengthen into leafy sprays;
Boughs where the thrush with crimson
   breast
Shall haunt, and sing, and hide her nest;
   We plant upon the sunny lea
A shadow for the noontide hour,
A shelter from the summer shower,
   When we plant the apple tree.

WILLIAM CULLEN BRYANT

Shared Talents

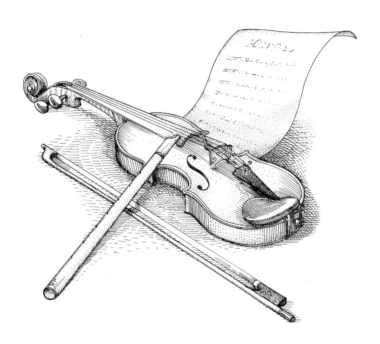

SOUND OF MUSIC

An old Hebrew legend says that after God created the world, He called the angels to Him and asked what they thought of it. One of them said, "There is something lacking; the sound of praise to the Creator." So God created music, and it was heard in the whisper of the wind, and in the song of the birds; and to man also was given the gift of song. And all down the ages this gift of song has indeed proved a blessing to multitudes of souls.

Chisel in hand stood a sculptor boy
  With his marble block before him,
And his eye lit up with a gleam of joy
  When his life dream passed before him.

He carved it well on the shapeless stone
  With many a sharp incision;
That angel dream he made his own,
  His own that angel vision.

GEORGE W. DOANE

Books are a series of windows opening on the strangeness of the world—the physical world, which we are finding more intricate than we ever dreamed; the world of emotions, which the novelist knows is of equal intricacy; and the world of the spirit, where all of us need as much light as we can get.

MARCHETTE CHUTE

It is the supreme art of the teacher to awaken joy in creative expression and knowledge.

ALBERT EINSTEIN

IDEALISM

If we stimulate a child's imagination to noble deeds and high resolves at the same time that we expose his ears to a specific piece of music and if we continue doing this on several subsequent occasions, the music will eventually cause him to think and act in an idealistic fashion even though we are no longer present to incite his imagination with words.

GEORGE W. CRANE

CORE OF JOY

My first thought about art, as a child, was that the artist brings something into the world that didn't exist before and that he does it without destroying something else. That still seems to me its central magic, its core of joy.

JOHN UPDIKE

Music expresses that which cannot remain silent.

VICTOR HUGO

GOSHEN

"How can you live in Goshen?"
Said a friend from afar,
"This wretched country town
Where folks talk little things all year,
And plant their cabbage by the moon!"
Said I:
"I do not live in Goshen,—
I eat here, sleep here, work here;
I live in Greece,
Where Plato taught,
And Phidias carved,
And Epictetus wrote.
I dwell in Rome,
Where Michelangelo wrought
In color, form, and mass;
Where Cicero penned immortal lines,
And Dante sang undying songs.
Think not my life is small
Because you see a puny place;
I have my books; I have my dreams;
A thousand souls have left for me
Enchantment that transcends
Both time and place.
And so I live in Paradise,
Not here."

EDGAR FRANK

The first business of education is to make sure that the discovery of one's self is reasonably complete.

WILLIAM J. TUCKER

Good art is like good cooking: it can be tasted, but not explained.

MAURICE DE VLAMINCK

Do all the good you can,
By all the means you can,
In all the places you can,
At all the times you can,
To all the people you can,
As long as ever you can.

JOHN WESLEY

Every individual is nature's creative experiment, trying out different ways of life in different environments.

THEODOSIUS DOBZHANSKY

He that climbs a ladder must begin at the first round.

SIR WALTER SCOTT

Kitchen Chatter

FULL MEASURE

It was a new recipe—but the same old metal measuring cup. A few dents here and there, the rim a little bent, the handle a bit wobbly, but reassuringly familiar in her hand. The dents were a reminder that it often had been a makeshift plaything, paired with a wooden spoon, for her children and grand-children. Her daughter had recently given her a set of brightly colored plastic mea-sures, but they held no memories.

She thought back over the years. How many times had the battered cup measured ingredients for her favorite recipes? Flour for bread she'd take out of the oven, crusty and fragrant—not the oven of the chrome and enamel electric stove she used now, but of the velvety black kitchen range that had a voracious appetite for cobs, wood, and oc-casional coal and had to be relieved daily of clogging ash.

The old cup had measured vast quantities of painstakingly prepared juice and sugar for jellies that through the years had lined the shelves in the "fruit cellar," their jewel-like colors ranging from pale pink to deep purple.

The cup had held tart red cherries for pie in summer, crisp juicy apple slices and golden pumpkin in the fall, nuts and fruits for cakes baked in November, anticipating happy Christmas reunions. It had helped with many a birthday cake for the young, the old, and the in-between. Now and then it had measured ingredients for a wedding cake, celebrating the start of another home where a shiny new measuring cup would help prepare good food for a rising gen-eration.

Some of her children were coming for dinner tonight. Smiling, she poured milk into the mixing bowl, then her worn fingers gently set the cup down. To all the other ingredients it had ever measured, she knew it had added love.

CHARLOTTE A. SWEDE

THE KITCHEN DOOR

Beyond my door the early day
begins with sunlit trees,
and robins hop the dewy grass
and ride the morning breeze.

I stand beside the open door
to greet a friend or two,
for afternoon is chatting time
and friendships to renew.

Then twilight shadows cross the walk,
and toward the kitchen door
come voices raised in happiness—
My family's home once more.

VIRGINIA COVEY BOSWELL

The time of business does not with me differ from the time of prayer; and in the noise and clutter of my kitchen, while several persons are at the same time calling for different things, I possess God in as great tranquility as if I were upon my knees before the blessed Sacrament.

BROTHER LAWRENCE

TEAMWORK

A splendid team, my wife and I;
She washes dishes, and I dry.
I sometimes pass her back a dish
To give another cleansing swish.
She sometimes holds up to the light
A glass I haven't dried just right.
But mostly there is no complaint,
Or it is courteous and faint,
For I would never care to see
The washing job consigned to me,
And though the things I dry still drip,
She keeps me for companionship.

RICHARD ARMOUR

There is no spectacle on earth more appealing than that of a beautiful woman in the act of cooking dinner for someone she loves.

THOMAS WOLFE

TOUCHING SHOULDERS

There's a comforting thought at the close of
the day,
When I'm weary and lonely and sad,
That sort of grips hold of my crusty old
heart
And bids it be merry and glad.
It gets in my soul and it drives out the
blues,
And finally thrills through and through.
It is just a sweet memory that chants the
refrain:
"I'm glad I touch shoulders with you!"

Did you know you were brave, did you
know you were strong?
Did you know there was one leaning hard?
Did you know that I waited and listened
and prayed,
And was cheered by your simplest word?
Did you know that I longed for that smile
on your face,
For the sound of your voice ringing true?
Did you know I grew stronger and better
because
I had merely touched shoulders with you?

I am glad that I live, that I battle and strive
For the place that I know I must fill;
I am thankful for sorrows, I'll meet with a
grin
What fortune may send, good or ill.
I may not have wealth, I may not be great,
But I know I shall always be true,
For I have in my life that courage you gave
When once I rubbed shoulders with you.

Every other book may be distrusted, but the purpose of a cookery book is unmistakable—to increase the happiness of mankind.

JOSEPH CONRAD

131

Table Talk

LISTENING

What you are doing when you are listening as a Christian is putting your hand quietly in the other person's life and feeling gently along the rim of his or her soul until you come to a crack, some frustration, some problem or anguish you sense that person may not be totally conscious of. As you are listening, you are loving this person and accepting him just as he is. The magic of this kind of concern is that you will often find your conversation moving imperceptibly from the general surface talk of the world situation and the weather into the intimate world of families and of hopes, of his life and yours. This change of climate sometimes takes place in a very short time in a listening atmosphere of concern and trust.

KEITH MILLER

A LITTLE MORE

Let me be a little kinder,
  Let me be a little blinder
To the faults of those about me;
  Let me praise a little more;
Let me be, when I am weary,
  Just a little bit more cheery;
Let me serve a little better
  Those that I am striving for.

Let me be a little braver
  When temptation bids me waver;
Let me strive a little harder
  To be all that I should be;
Let me be a little meeker
  With the brother that is weaker;
Let me think more of my neighbor
  And a little less of me.

O Lord, let me ever take one bite at every meal in memory of thee.

MALTBIE DAVENPORT BABCOCK

TABLE GRACE

We bless and thank thee, dear God, that these friends are welcomed to our family circle today. May our understanding, appreciation, and love for one another grow in grace, deepen in meaning, and become a rich blessing as we break this bread in thy holy name.

The table is really the family altar! Here those of all ages come together and help to sustain both their physical and their spiritual existence. If a sacrament is "an actual conveyance of spiritual meaning and power by a material process," then a family meal can be a sacrament. It entwines the material and the spiritual in a remarkable way. The food, in and of itself, is purely physical, but it represents both labor and love in its production and it represents human service in its use. Here, at one common table, is the father who has earned, the mother who has prepared or planned, and the children who share, according to need, whatever their antecedent participation may have been.

ELTON TRUEBLOOD

A dining room table with children's eager, hungry faces around it ceases to be a mere dining room table and becomes an altar.

SIMEON STRUNSKY

GRACE AT EVENING

Be with us, Lord, at eventide;
  Far has declined the day,
Our hearts have glowed
Along the road,
  Thou hast made glad our way.

Take Thou this loaf and bless it, Lord,
  And then with us partake;
Unveil our eyes
To recognize
  Thyself, for Thy dear sake.

EDWIN McNEILL POTEAT

From THE GOLDEN LEGEND

A holy family, that make
Each meal a Supper of the Lord.

HENRY WADSWORTH LONGFELLOW

Thou that hast given so much to me,
Give one thing more—a grateful heart;
Not thankful when it pleaseth me,
As if Thy blessings had spare days;
But such a heart, whose pulse may be
Thy praise.

GEORGE HERBERT

We thank thee, Father, for thy care
And for thy bounty everywhere.
For food and every other gift
Our grateful hearts to thee we lift.

ANIMAL CRACKERS

Animal crackers, and cocoa to drink,
That is the finest of suppers, I think;
When I'm grown up and can have what I
    please
I think I shall always insist upon these.
What do you choose when you're offered a
    treat?
When Mother says, "What would you like
    best to eat?"
Is it waffles and syrup, or cinnamon toast?
It's cocoa and animals that I love most!

CHRISTOPHER MORLEY

AN OLD ENGLISH PRAYER

Give us, Lord, a bit of sun, a bit of work, a
bit ot fun. Give us in all struggle and sput-
ter our daily bread, a bit of butter. Give us
health, our keep to make, a bit to spare for
others' sake. Give us, too, a bit of song, a
tale or book to help us along. Give us, Lord,
a chance to be our goodly best—brave, wise
and free—our goodly best for ourselves and
others, 'til all men learn to live as brothers.

Thankful Hearts

Something happens when the members of a family lift their hearts to God in prayer together, when each member takes his turn in voicing to God the deepest yearning of his soul for each of them and all of them. Something happens when the members of a family read the Bible together, when they discuss the Christian faith together, when they speak together of the life which God wants each of them to live.

ROY PEARSON

PRAYER

Lord, behold our family here assembled. We thank Thee for this place in which we dwell; for the love that unites us; for the peace accorded us this day; for the hope with which we expect the morrow; for the health, the work, the food, and the bright skies that make our lives delightful; for our friends in all parts of the earth.

Give us grace and strength to forbear and to persevere. Give us courage and gaiety and the quiet mind. Spare to us our friends, soften to us our enemies. Bless us, if it may be, in all our innocent endeavors. If it may not, give us strength to encounter that which is to come, that we may be brave in peril, constant in tribulation, temperate in wrath and in all changes of fortune, and down to the gates of death, loyal and loving to one another.

ROBERT LOUIS STEVENSON

The God to whom little boys say their prayers has a face very like their mother's.

JAMES M. BARRIE

THANKFULNESS

My God, I thank Thee who hast made
  The earth so bright;
So full of splendor and of joy,
  Beauty and light;
So many glorious things are here,
  Noble and right!

ADELAIDE A. PROCTER

God has two dwellings—one in heaven and the other in a thankful heart.

IZAAK WALTON

PRAYER FOR A LITTLE GIRL

Now I lay her down to sleep;
I pray Thee, Lord, her soul to keep.
I pray Thee, Lord, her beauty guard
As violets in a grassy yard.
I pray Thee, keep her goodness bright
As little finches in their flight.
God bless her wants; let her design
Them into ways that follow Thine.
All this I ask for Christ's own sake.
Before her soul again You take
May she bend over a small bed
And pray with joy, as I have prayed.

ANN OSBORNE

A PRAYER FOR PARENTS

O God, Heavenly Father, we pray Thee, by Thy Fatherhood, to teach the hearts of parents. Give them wisdom and patience. Help them to know what to grant and what to deny. Deliver them alike from foolish fondness and from aimless harshness. Through the memory of Thy love, give them such an understanding heart as may shun all partiality and may discover and foster every seed of goodness. Make them glad to cooperate with all means of education and growth which state and church provide. Help them humbly and wisely to surrender their children to the larger claims of life in the service of their fellow men. May their faith in Thy love to their children and in childhood's share in the kingdom be the power by which young hearts shall be made strong. Through their own childlikeness may they learn to show to their children the way into Thine everlasting kingdom.

Holy Spirit of God, come among us.
Come as the wind and cleanse us,
Come as the fire and burn,
Come as the dew and refresh us,
Come as the dawn and illuminate.
Convict, convert, and consecrate
Our hearts and lives, for your glory
And for the good of your church,
Through Christ our Lord.

A CHILD'S PRAYER

Make me, dear Lord, polite and kind
To every one, I pray.
And may I ask you how you find
Yourself, dear Lord, today?

JOHN BANNISTER TABB

For the glory of the morning,
For the starry rest of night,
For light, and life, and love, and mind,
God's fullness of delight,
We would bring as our thanksgiving
   A true and open heart
And the wish that in God's beauty
   We too may be a part.

Prayer is the soul's sincere desire,
   Uttered or unexpressed;
The motion of a hidden fire,
   That trembles in the breast.

Prayer is the burden of a sigh,
   The falling of a tear;
The upward glancing of an eye,
   When none but God is near.

Prayer is the simplest form of speech
   That infant lips can try;
Prayer, the sublimest strains that reach
   The Majesty on high.

O Thou by whom we come to God—
   The Life, the Truth, the Way!
The path of prayer Thyself has trod;
   Lord, teach us how to pray!

JAMES MONTGOMERY

AN IRISH BLESSING

May the blessing of light be on you, light from without and light from within. May the blessed sunlight shine on you and warm your heart till it glows like a great peat fire so that the stranger may come and warm himself at it and also be a friend.

And may the light shine out of the two eyes of you like a candle set in the windows of a house, bidding the wanderer to come in out of the storm.

And may the blessing of the rain be on you—the soft sweet rain. May it fall upon your spirit so that all the little flowers may spring up and shed their sweetness on the air.

And may the blessing of the great rains be upon you. May they beat upon your spirit and wash it fair and clean, and have it shine like a shining pool where the blue of heaven shines reflected, and sometimes a star.

And may the blessing of the earth be on you—the great and round earth. May you ever have a kindly greeting for them you pass as you're going along the roads. May the earth be soft under you when you lay upon it, tired at the end of the day, and may it rest so lightly over you that your soul may be quickly up and through it, and up, and off, and on its way to God.

PRAYER

Build me a son, O Lord, who will be strong enough to know when he is weak, and brave enough to face himself when he is afraid; one who will be proud and unbending in honest defeat, and humble and gentle in victory.

Build me a son whose heart will be clear, whose goal will be high; a son who will master himself before he seeks to master other men; one who will learn to laugh, yet never forget how to weep; one who will reach into the future, yet never forget the past.

And after all these things are his, add, I pray, enough of a sense of humor, so that he may always be serious, yet never take himself too seriously. Give him humility, so that he may always remember the simplicity of true greatness, the open mind of true wisdom, the meekness of true strength.

Then I, his father, will dare to whisper, "I have not lived in vain."

DOUGLAS MacARTHUR

A mother's prayers, silent and gentle, can never miss the road to the throne of all bounty.

HENRY WARD BEECHER

Children have more need of models than of critics.

JOSEPH JOUBERT

God, help me to look upon a little child as though he were I. Help me to remember that he is human. That fatigue envelops him and boredom gets him down. That he has temptations like unto those I had or might have had when I was his age. He wants to follow me, but I walk such devious pathways that my intentions are beyond him.

Save him from my unruly temper when I have not had enough sleep. Keep him from my hand of wrath when I am on edge.

Preserve him from my outbursts of anger when my own life has been shattered. Help me to put the pieces back together quickly lest I hurt him.

Make up the deficits which come from my insolent ways. Let him not be held accountable for my shoddy methods of living nor from my lack of interest in him.

Hide from him my sham and pretense, my efforts to stand well in his eyes, and my labor to show forth my knowledge.

Help me never to forget that I am guiding tomorrow's parents. Don't let me blight them with a hurt which will show unto the third and fourth generations.

And when the shadows lengthen at nightfall, when the busy world is hushed by the twilight, and darkness falls across the face of the deep, grant me that peace which only Thy children possess.

For our bodies, quick and strong,
Thee to serve the whole day long:
For the power to think and know,
For the will like thee to grow;
For the good by which we live,
Father, thanks to thee we give.

Parents are not obligated to give their children a secure future, but they are obligated to give them a secure foundation on which to build their future.

RALPH W. SOCKMAN

PRAYER

Almighty God, our Father, we thank You for our home and pray that You will bless all who live within this family circle. We are grateful for Your mercies which daily attend our days—for food, clothing and shelter, for the warmth of our affection and for the ties that bind us together.

Help us so to live each day and so to love one another that we may never be afraid or ashamed but always may our hearts be happy, our thoughts good, our words gentle, our deeds genuine and our hands ready to help.

Daily renew our strength, replenish our love and restore our faith that we may face life bravely because we face it together. On this family reunion day deepen our love for one another and for You that love may reign in every room in our hearts and rule in every room in our home.

EDWARD G. LATCH

Christian Life Experiences

_____

made a commitment to Christ on _____

_____

made a commitment to Christ on _____

_____

made a commitment to Christ on _____

_____

Photographs

The Family Altar

A Christian home means a home where Christ is known and loved and served; where children come to know Him through their parents; where Christian training of children is placed ahead of the social ambition of the mother and the business ambition of the father; where the father is determined to carry on his business in conformity with the mind of Christ; where both father and mother are determined to make their social life conform to high Christian ideals; and where eyes see far horizons of a world to be won for Christ.

PAUL CALVIN PAYNE

SPECIAL GUESTS

God is love. He created this magnificent world and then, in love, called us to share it with Him. Because each of us is His special guest, He created each of us uniquely. Just ask the mother of identical twins how she tells them apart, and she will say, "Oh, that's easy—they're so different." Love is celebrating the uniqueness of each of us.

VIRGINIA McEWAN

Anyone can build an altar; it requires a God to provide the flame. Anybody can build a house; we need the Lord for the creation of a home.

JOHN HENRY JOWETT

A STEEPLE ON THE HOUSE

What if it should turn out eternity
Was but the steeple on our house of life
That made our house of life a house of
    worship?
We do not go up there to sleep at night
We do not go up there to live by day.
Nor need we go up there to live.
A spire and belfry coming on the roof
Means that a soul is coming on the flesh.

ROBERT FROST

The Christian home is the Master's workshop where the processes of character-molding are silently, lovingly, faithfully and successfully carried on.

RICHARD MONCKTON MILNES

In the breast of a bulb
Is the promise of spring;
In the little blue egg
Is a bird that will sing;
In the soul of a seed
Is the hope of the sod;
In the heart of a child
Is the Kingdom of God.

WILLIAM L. STIDGER

From MY ALTAR

I have worshipped in churches and chapels;
   I've prayed in the busy street;
I have sought my God and have found him
   Where the waves of his ocean beat;
I have knelt in the silent forest
   In the shade of some ancient tree;
But the dearest of all my altars
   Was raised at my mother's knee.
JOHN H. STYLES, JR.

Fundamentally Jesus was childlike in an unchildlike world, and this made him then and now a stranger.
SAMUEL H. MILLER

O blessed house, where man and wife, united
   In Thy true love, have both one heart and mind,
Where both to Thy salvation are invited,
   And in Thy doctrine both contentment find;
Where both, to Thee, in truth, for ever cleaving
   In joy, in grief, make Thee their only stay,
And fondly hope in Thee to be believing,
   Both in the good and in the evil day.
KARL JOHANN PHILIPP SPITTA,
TRANSLATED BY CHARLES WILLIAM SCHAEFFER

Let every father and mother realize that when their child is three years of age, they have done more than half they will ever do for its character.
HORACE BUSHNELL

Our families in Thine arms enfold
As Thou didst keep Thy folk of old.
OLIVER WENDELL HOLMES

The only religion that is any good is home-made religion.
PAUL CALVIN PAYNE

PRAYER

The morning is the gate of day,
   But ere you enter there
See that you set to guard it well,
   The sentinel of prayer.

So shall God's grace your steps attend,
   But nothing else pass through
Save what can give the countersign;
   The Father's will for you.

When you have reached the end of day
   Where night and sleep await,
Set there the sentinel again
   To bar the evening's gate.

So shall no fear disturb your rest,
   No danger and no care.
For only peace and pardon pass
   The watchful guard of prayer.

We build an altar here, and pray
  That Thou wilt show Thy face.
Dear Lord, if Thou wilt come to stay.
This home we consecrate to-day
  Will be a Holy Place.

LOUIS F. BENSON

A HOUSEWIFE'S PRAYER

My loving Lord, my constant friend,
Since I've no time to be
A saint by doing lovely things
Like witnessing for Thee,
Or singing joyous praises
That rise to heaven's gates,
Make me a saint by getting meals
And cleaning up the plates!

Although I must have Martha's hands
I still have Mary's mind,
And in my quiet kitchen
I think of Thee, so kind,
Preparing food for hungry men
By Galilee's blue shore;
Accept this meditation, Lord,
I haven't time for more!

Light all the kitchen with Thy love,
And fill it with Thy peace;
Forgive my foolish, anxious care,
And make my striving cease.
Thou who did love to give men food
In cot or by the sea,
Accept this service that I do;
I do it unto Thee!

HILDUR SHEADY CHRISTENSEN

A home without God is like a house without
a roof.

HORACE BUSHNELL

ADORATION

If I but had a little coat,
A coat to fit a no-year old,
I'd button it close about His throat
To cover Him from the cold,
  The cold,
To cover Him from the cold.

If my heart were a shining coin,
A silver coin or a coin of gold,
Out of my side I'd it purloin
And give it to Him to hold,
  To hold,
And give it to Him to hold.

If my heart were a house also,
A house also with room to spare,
I never would suffer my Lord to go
Homeless, but house Him there,
  Oh there,
Homeless, but house Him there.

BYRON HERBERT REECE

He is happiest, be he king or peasant, who
finds peace in his home.

GOETHE

The aim of education is to make it natural
for men to talk about God.

NATHAN PUSEY

148

AFTER THE CRUCIFIXION

We were the children Jesus loved.
Jonathan sat upon His knee
That morning in the marketplace
Of Galilee.

Benjamin was the little boy
Who had the lunch of fish and bread
Which Jesus blessed—and Benjamin saw
Five thousand fed.

And Miriam was sick, and slept
And would not wake—and she can tell
How Jesus came and took her hand,
And she was well!

We were all children, everywhere,
Who looked upon His face. We knew,
That day they told us He had died,
It was not true.

We wondered why our parents wept
And doubted Him and were deceived,
For we remembered what He said,
And we believed!

SARA HENDERSON HAY

When home is ruled according to God's word, angels might be asked to stay with us, and they would not find themselves out of their element.

CHARLES H. SPURGEON

Faith makes the uplook good, the outlook bright, the inlook favorable, and the future glorious.

V. RAYMOND EDMAN

The best way to train up a child the way he should go is to travel that road occasionally yourself.

JOSH BILLINGS

A CRADLE HYMN

Hush! my dear, lie still and slumber,
    Holy angels guard thy bed!
Heavenly blessings without number
    Gently falling on thy head.

Sleep, my babe; thy food and raiment,
    House and home, thy friends provide;
All without thy care or payment:
    All thy wants are well supplied.

ISAAC WATTS

The greatest work any of us can do for another, whether old or young, is to teach the soul to draw its water from the wells of God.

F. B. MEYER

SANCTUARY

On sunlit hills where joy is,
In the heart of the wood where calm is,
In little homes where love is,
In all the world where weary souls seek,
Eager and wistful, their tryst to keep,
There is God, and sanctuary.

GRACE A. AURINGER

Baptisms

_____ was baptized on _____

by _____

at _____

_____ was baptized on _____

by _____

at _____

_____ was baptized on _____

by _____

at _____

_____ was baptized on _____

by _____

at _____

_____ was baptized on _____

by _____

at _____

_____ was baptized on _____

by _____

at _____

Photographs

To Love and Serve Him

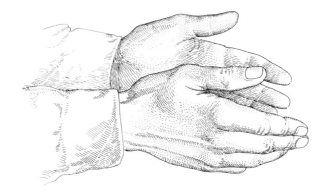

THE CHURCH BAZAAR

The little church upon the village green
Had held its annual bazaar
And through its friendly open doors, the
    lights
Sent golden shafts that pierced the falling
    night.
The women hurrying home were laden
    down
With treasures from the booths where had
    been found
A marvelous array of things, enticingly
    displayed
Many of which were fearfully and wonder-
    fully made.
A great success, this annual event,
For which each gladly worked and freely
    spent
So altogether weary, they were well content
And felt the satisfaction worthy efforts
    bring.
Besides, the church could have new carpets
    in the spring.

ESTHER ANDERSON ORDWAY

Go your way in peace.
Be of good courage.
Hold fast to that which is good;
Render to no man evil for evil.
Strengthen the fainthearted,
Support the weak,
Help and cheer the sick,
Honor all men,
Love and serve the Lord;
And may the blessing of God
Be upon you and remain with you forever.

GLOUCESTER CATHEDRAL

WORSHIP

Worship is seeing the incomprehensible
vastness of the ocean and believing that
God is of greater magnitude.

Worship is climbing a mountain with
faith to reach the top.

Worship is stopping to listen to the song
of a bird.

Worship is looking upward with the posi-
tive awareness that God is greater than the
beautiful universe.

Worship is the thrill of planting a seed in
the garden and rejoicing when it begins to
grow.

Worship is to open the heart and become
full of the glory of the Lord.

Worship is to open the soul for commu-
nion with God.

Worship is the act of opening the shutter
of one's whole self, taking a picture of God,
and letting the whole being respond to
divine love and blessing.

Worship is to be another wise man, with
the chief desire and goal of finding the
Christ, and kneeling upon the holy ground
to praise him.

Worship is to be another wise man and
know the need of satisfying the inner, calling desire of the heart to look up and recognize the one great Power of the universe.

HAROLD A. SCHULZ

WORSHIP THE LORD

Worship the Lord in the beauty of
    holiness,
Bow down before Him, His glory
    proclaim;
Gold of obedience, and incense of
    lowliness,
Kneel and adore Him, —the Lord is
    His name.

Low at His feet lay thy burden of
    carefulness,
High on His heart He will bear it for thee,
Comfort thy sorrows, and answer thy
    prayerfulness,
Guiding thy steps as may best for thee be.

Truth in its beauty, and love in its
    tenderness,
These are the offerings we lay on His
    shrine;
These, though we bring them in trembling
    and fearfulness,
He will accept in the Name all divine.

                JOHN S. B. MONSELL

SMALL SUNS AND HALOS

Sixty days of drought this summer,
Scarcely a flower shows its face.
Rally Day the coming Sunday,
. . . Nothing for the altar place.

Mothers, searching stunted gardens,
Colors once stood there in rows,
Find no lilies, tall, religious,
No aristocratic rose.

Small boys, wiser than their parents,
Trudge out barefoot to the farms,
Gather small suns with white halos,
Stem by green stem in their arms.

Sunday comes all hot and thirsty,
Yet the church breathes fresh and sweet;
Daisies, bunched in praying fountains
Cool away the summer heat.

                RALPH W. SEAGER

There is no substitute for Christian parents.
Before the church can make itself strong in
the nation and the world, it must make
itself significant in the home.

              LAWRENCE O. LINEBERGER

THE ANGEL WITH THE BAND AID

Choir cherubs move down the aisle;
Their solemn faces show no smile.
Holding their hands as if in prayer,
They're walking slowly, taking care
That they don't stumble as they walk;
Of course 'twould be quite wrong to talk.
As one little chorister passes me,
On her prayerful hands I chance to see
A Band Aid covering her fingertip
And her choir robe sporting a tiny rip.
Then my wandering mind is filled with
    mirth
As I think, "These angels are of Earth."

                 BONNIE DARSIE

The church is the family of God. It is seen in miniature in each family. The impulse which sends us to worship together as a church should send us to worship together as a family.

                 JOHN FERGUSON

GOD'S HOUSE

If you have not felt that God is present here, and that you are before him, then your visit to God's house has been in vain. For all else that you have seen and heard has been of no consequence, and you might just as well have remained at home. For certainly this place is God's house—and yet your own house should also become a house of God.

             SØREN KIERKEGAARD

We had from childhood not only the experience of love and truth common to all family life, but the idea of them embodied in the person of Jesus, a picture always present to our imagination as well as our feelings.

                 JOYCE CARY

Living by the Word

When I am reading a book, whether wise or silly, it seems to me to be alive and talking to me.

JONATHAN SWIFT

We search the world for truth. We cull
The good, the true, the beautiful,
From graven stone and written scroll,
And all old flower-fields of the soul;
And, weary seekers of the best,
We come back laden from our quest,
To find that all the sages said
Is in the Book our mothers read.

JOHN GREENLEAF WHITTIER

BOOKS

They are landmarks and guides in our journey through life. They are pegs and loops on which we can hang up, or from which we can take down, at pleasure, the wardrobe of a moral imagination, the relics of our best affections, the tokens and records of our happiest hours.

CLIFTON FADIMAN

When we teach a child to read, our primary aim is not to enable it to decipher a waybill or receipt, but to kindle its imagination, enlarge its vision, and open for it the avenues of knowledge.

CHARLES W. ELIOT

THE BOOK OF BOOKS

Within this ample volume lies
The mystery of mysteries.
Happiest they of human race
To whom their God has given grace
To read, to fear, to hope, to pray,
To lift the latch, to force the way;
But better had they ne'er been born
That read to doubt or read to scorn.

SIR WALTER SCOTT

Any individual or institution that could take the Bible to every home in this country would do more for the country than all the armies from the beginning of our history to the present time.

DAVID J. BREWER

Give me a used Bible and I will, I think, be able to tell you about a man by the places that are edged with the dirt of seeking fingers.

JOHN STEINBECK

The Bible does not say very much about homes. It says a great deal about the things that make them. It speaks about life and love and joy and peace and rest. If we get a house and put these into it, we shall have secured a home.

JOHN HENRY JOWETT

Hold fast to the Bible as the sheet anchor of your liberties. To the influence of this book we are indebted for the progress made, and to it we must look as our guide for the future.

ULYSSES S. GRANT

If you blot out from your life all that is taken from the sacred book, what would be left to bind society together?

BENJAMIN HARRISON

A real book is not one that we read but one that reads us.

W. H. AUDEN

Every man who knows how to read has it in his power to magnify himself, to multiply the ways in which he exists, to make his life full, significant, and interesting.

ALDOUS HUXLEY

The essential purpose of Christian education is to enable men to ask fundamental questions.

D. R. DAVIES

THE BIBLE

It is impossible to govern the world without the Bible.

GEORGE WASHINGTON

The best book which God has given to man.

ABRAHAM LINCOLN

The Bible is the word of life.

WOODROW WILSON

It is the support of the strong and the consolation of the weak; the dependence of organized government and the foundation of religion.

CALVIN COOLIDGE

The Bible—the rock upon which our republic rests.

ANDREW JACKSON

There is no other book so full of concentrated wisdom. As a nation we are indebted to the Book of Books for our national ideals and represented institutions.

HERBERT HOOVER

The Bible is the cornerstone of liberty.

THOMAS JEFFERSON

Home Is Where Love Abides

WHEN THE HEART IS FULL OF LOVE

There is beauty in the forest
When the trees are green and fair,
There is beauty in the meadow
When wild flowers scent the air.
There is beauty in the sunlight
And the soft blue beams above.
Oh, the world is full of beauty
When the heart is full of love.

ROCKER FULL OF LOVE

This cherry rocker; once it held
my grandmother, who cared
to rock her daughter with a song,
who knew love's joy is shared.

My mother soothed me in this chair
with gentle, loving arms;
and told me of the wondrous world,
and kept me safe from harm.

My own small daughter asks to rock.
She chants her homemade rhyme,
so snugly wrapped, in that dear chair,
with love that transcends time.

VIRGINIA COVEY BOSWELL

The home atmosphere is far different when a family stops trying to walk alone, when it sees its place in the bigger scheme of things. It works together for the things it can control, and trusts its God for guidance in problems beyond its control. Such a family can't help feeling closer together, more sure of itself, happier.

REFORMED CHURCH BULLETIN

We should so live and labor in our time so that which came to us as seed may go to the next generation as blossom, and that which came to us as blossom may go to them as fruit.

HENRY WARD BEECHER

IKE WALTON'S PRAYER

I crave, dear Lord,
No boundless hoard
  Of gold and gear,
  Nor jewels fine
  Nor lands, nor kine,
  Nor treasure-heaps of anything.
    Let but a little hut be mine
  Where at the hearthstone I may hear
    The cricket sing,
    And have the shine
  Of one glad woman's eyes to make,
  For my poor sake,
  Our simple home a place divine;
Just the wee cot—the cricket's chirr—
Love, and the smiling face of her.

JAMES WHITCOMB RILEY

To know when school is out that there is a place to go where there is shelter from the rain and the snow is a benediction to a youngster growing toward maturity. It undergirds him with a dependable base from which he can make his excursions into the unknown. If, now and then, he feels like running away, even the running is made tolerable by the possibility of turning back.

HAROLD BLAKE WALKER

There is nothing mightier or nobler than where man and wife are one heart and one mind in a house.

HOMER

I would give up all my genius, and all my books, if there were only some woman, somewhere, who cared whether or not I came home late for dinner.

IVAN TURGENEV

I want to thank Thee, Father,
For the fragrances of home;
The spiciness of gingerbread,
The sunny smell of clothes just off the line,
The children's hair
Clean from fresh shampooing,
The coziness of moth balls
As the winter clothes
Are taken from their trunks.

MYRA SCOVEL

Home is where life makes up its mind.

HAZEN G. WERNER

LOVE

Love is a circle that doth restless move
In the same sweet eternity of Love.

ROBERT HERRICK

The greatest of all arts is the art of living together.

WILLIAM LYON PHELPS

SONG FOR A LITTLE HOUSE

I'm glad our house is a little house,
Not too tall nor too wide;
I'm glad the hovering butterflies
Feel free to come inside.

Our little house is a friendly house,
It is not shy or vain;
It gossips with the talking trees
And makes friends with the rain.

And quick leaves cast a shimmer of green
Against our whited walls;
And in the phlox, the courteous bees
Are paying duty calls.

CHRISTOPHER MORLEY

I live in a constant endeavour to fence against the infirmities of ill health, and other evils of life, by mirth; being firmly persuaded that every time a man smiles, but much more so when he laughs, that it adds something to this Fragment of Life.

LAURENCE STERNE

Places We Have Lived

Photographs

Photographs

Photographs

Vacation Fun

OUT IN THE FIELDS WITH GOD

The little cares that fretted me,
  I lost them yesterday,
Among the fields above the sea,
  Among the winds at play,
Among the lowing of the herds,
  The rustling of the trees,
Among the singing of the birds,
  The humming of the bees.

The foolish fears of what might pass
  I cast them all away
Among the clover-scented grass
  Among the new-mown hay,
Among the rustling of the corn
  Where drowsy poppies nod,
Where ill thoughts die and good are born—
  Out in the fields with God!

Attributed to ELIZABETH BARRETT BROWNING

SUMMER RECIPE

Take one large, grassy field; one-half dozen children; two or three small dogs; a pinch of brook and some pebbles. Mix well the children and the dogs together, put them into the field, stirring constantly. Pour the brook over the pebbles, sprinkle the field with flowers; spread over all a deep blue sky and bake in the hot sun. When brown, remove and set away to cool in the bathtub.

SUNSHINE MAGAZINE

School is over,
  Oh, what fun!
Lessons finished,
  Play begun.
Who'll run fastest,
  You or I?
Who'll laugh loudest?
  Let us try.

KATE GREENAWAY

NATURE'S CREED

I believe in the brook as it wanders
  From hillside into glade;
I believe in the breeze as it whispers
  When evening's shadows fade.
I believe in the roar of the river
  As it dashes from high cascade;
I believe in the cry of the tempest
'Mid the thunder's cannonade.
I believe in the light of shining stars,
  I believe in the sun and the moon;
I believe in the flash of lightening,
  I believe in the night-bird's croon.
I believe in the faith of the flowers,
  I believe in the rock and sod,
For in all of these appeareth clear
  The handiwork of God.

VACATION

The blessed Heavenly Father knew
That there come times to laborers true,
That they must hide away and rest—
And so He made the mountain crest,
The quiet little fishing nook,
Where work and care would have to look
A long, long time before they'd find
The ones who hid away behind
The drooping birch and scented pine.

RUTH SMELTZER

FISHING

To go fishing is the chance to wash one's
soul with pure air, with the rush of the
brook, or with the shimmer of the sun on
blue water. It brings meekness and inspiration from the decency of nature, charity
toward tackle-makers, patience toward
fish, a mockery of profits and egos, a quiet-
ing of hate, a rejoicing that you do not have
to decide a darned thing until next week.
And it is discipline in the equality of men—
for all men are equal before fish.

HERBERT HOOVER

FOURTH OF JULY NIGHT

Pin wheels whirling round
Spit sparks upon the ground,
And rockets shoot up high
And blossom in the sky—
Blue and yellow, green and red
Flowers falling on my head,
And I don't ever have to go
To bed, to bed, to bed!

DOROTHY ALDIS

Photographs

Photographs

Photographs

Deepening Our Friendships

To have a friend is to have one of the sweetest gifts; to be a friend is to experience solemn and tender education of soul from day to day.

A friend remembers us when we have forgotten ourselves. A friend takes loving heed of our work, our health, our aims, and our plans. He may rebuke us, and we are not angry. If he is silent, we understand.

A friend must forget much, forgive much, forbear much. Friendship costs time, affection, strength, patience, love. Sometimes a man must lay down his life for his friend. There cannot be true friendship without self-sacrifice.

We may be slow to make friends, but having once made them neither life nor death, misunderstanding, distance nor doubt must ever come between.

Friendships are the fruits gathered from trees planted in the rich soil of love and nurtured with tender care and understanding.

ALMA L. WEIXELBAUM

From WALKING WITH SOMEONE

The thermometer reading
  Was right above eight
When our girl left the house
  At a speeded-up gait
So's to join with a friend
  Who was just going by.
When I warned of the cold,
  I received a reply
Rather wise for a child
  Not eleven years old,
"When you're walking with someone,
  It isn't so cold!"

MARGARET RORKE

DOORBELLS

You never know with a doorbell
  Who may be ringing it—
It may be Great-Aunt Cynthia
  To spend the day and knit;

It may be a peddler with things to sell
  (I'll buy some when I'm older),
Or the grocer's boy with his apron on
  And a basket on his shoulder;

It may be the old umbrella man
  Giving his queer, cracked call,
Or a lady dressed in rustly silk,
  With a card case and parasol.

Doorbells are like a magic game,
  Or the grab bag at a fair—
You never know when you hear one ring
  Who may be waiting there.

RACHEL FIELD

A friend is a present you give yourself.

ROBERT LOUIS STEVENSON

A good neighbor doubles the value of a house.

GERMAN PROVERB

A friendly person can make a strange place seem like home.

PATRICIA F. ROSS

A near neighbor is more important than a remote relative.

CHINESE PROVERB

Every soul that touches yours—
Be it the slightest contact—
Gets therefrom some good;
Some little grace; one kindly thought;
One aspiration yet unfelt;
One bit of courage
For the darkening sky;
One gleam of faith
To brace the thickening ills of life;
One glimpse of brighter skies—
To make this life worth while
And heaven a surer heritage.

GEORGE ELIOT

POST OFFICE MIRACLE

The rain
Is drumming on dead leaves today,
Dismally.

Dripping eaves and creaking door—
Muddy boot tracks on the floor—
Dull, ugly, postered wall . . .

Key right to four and left to three:
An envelope addressed to me
In dear, familiar scrawl . . .

The rain
Is dancing on red leaves today,
Joyously.

MYRNA HAIGHT

No one has so big a house that he does not need a good neighbor.

SWEDISH PROVERB

Come in the evening, or come in the
  morning,
Come when you're looked for, or
  come without warning,
Kisses and welcome you'll find here
  before you,
And the oftener you come here the more
  I'll adore you.

THOMAS O. DAVIS

SMILE

Like a bread without the spreadin',
  Like a puddin' without sauce,
Like a mattress without beddin',
  Like a cart without a hoss,
Like a door without a latch-string,
  Like a fence without a stile,
Like a dry an' barren creek bed—
  Is the face without a smile.

Like a house without a dooryard,
  Like a yard without a flower,
Like a clock without a main spring,
  That will never tell the hour;
A thing that sort of makes you feel
  A hunger all the while—
Oh, the saddest sight that ever was
  Is a face without a smile!

I have three chairs in my house: one for solitude, two for friendship, three for company.

HENRY DAVID THOREAU

Widening Circles

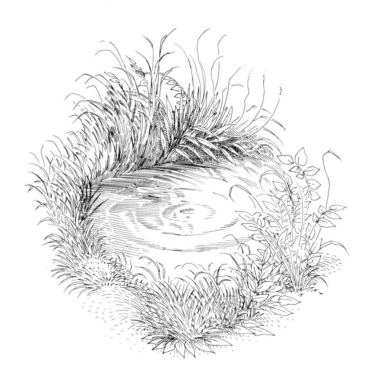

BUILD ME A HOUSE

Build me a house with windows,
  With windows everywhere!
Through which may stream God's golden
    light
  And flower-sweet air.

And let my house of windows
  Front towards the dawning day,
That I may see the sun each morning
  Start on his way.

Build me a house with windows
  Some facing south and north,
So I may watch migrating birds
  As they wind forth.

Build me a house with windows
  Looking far to the west,
Then I can see each rose-crowned day
  Go down to rest.

Build high and wide these windows
  That broad my vision be.
Oh, shut not a world of wonder
  Away from me!

AGNES MacCARTHY HICKEY

Her kitchen's the busiest place in the house
  And the cheeriest place of all,
A stove, and a sink, and a washing machine,
  And a map of the world on the wall.

KATHERINE PARKER

When an American says that he loves his country, he means not only that he loves the New England hills, the prairies glistening in the sun, the wide and rising plains, the great mountains and the sea. He means that he loves an inner air, an inner light in which freedom lives and in which a man can draw the breath of self-respect.

ADLAI STEVENSON

The home is a lighthouse which has the lamp of God on the table and the light of Christ in the window to give guidance to those who wander in darkness.

HENRY RISCHE

182

The concept of the family of God widens in concentric circles as the biblical account unfolds. As it widens, it deepens. In the Old Testament, we read of a covenant people who stand in a peculiar relation to God: first a man, then a family, a clan, and a nation. Participation in the common privileges was determined by blood and sealed by the rite of circumcision. In the New Testament, the horizon widens to include all mankind, and the more intimate figure of the family is used to describe the relations of the members to one another and to God the Father.

WILLIAM DOUGLAS CHAMBERLAIN

To a man in a spacecraft coming back from the moon or Mars the entire earth will look like home.

EUGENE G. FUBINI

I stand before the map of the world; before its countries stretched wide and its waters deep. I stand before the rivers lying like long crooked fingers across the land, fed forever from the streams, the snows and the rains of the mountains, pouring endlessly into the seas.

Up and down the rivers people have their mansions and their squatted huts. Children are born and families fish the waters for food, or till the soil of the valleys and countrysides. Some families work in factories and some in the dark interior of the earth.

How alike we are around the world; living in our families, working and playing, having fun and having sorrow, knowing fear and security, needing food and clothing.

On this day I send into families of the world my wishes for good will. I will make room in my heart for all my brothers and sisters everywhere.

ABBIE GRAHAM

O mothers of the world, I lift this cry
Of honor to your name. But in my heart
There is another cry;
That each of you be mother to all babes;
Share in a universal motherhood;
Reach out your hands to every child in
        need.
Even as the Christ commanded, when of old
He would make all of us one family,
Reach out your hearts in love,
Becoming hands and feet and lips for God.

EDWIN MARKHAM

He who prays for his neighbor will be heard for himself.

HEBREW PROVERB

If a man be gracious and courteous to strangers, it shows he is a citizen of the world, and that his heart is no island cut off from other lands, but a continent that joins them.

FRANCIS BACON

Families must accept their citizenship in their community, nation, and world as the context in which their lives are lived. The home cannot be thought of as an island of happiness that exists in isolation from the tumultuous world of change. The home bounces around in the tumult, feels the tension, shares the sadness and hope of that whole world.

JOHN R. FRY

What the best and wisest parent wants for his own child that must the community want for all its children.

JOHN DEWEY

If there be some weaker one,
Give me strength to help him on;
If a blinder soul there be,
Let me guide him nearer Thee.
Make my mortal dreams come true
With the work I fain would do;
Clothe with life the weak intent,
Let me be the thing I meant;
Let me find in Thy employ
Peace that dearer is than joy;
Out of self to love be led
And to heaven acclimated,
Until all things sweet and good
Seem my natural habitude.

JOHN GREENLEAF WHITTIER

ON BEING YOU

You do not belong to you. You belong to the universe. The significance of you will remain forever obscure to you, but you may assume you are fulfilling your significance if you apply yourself to converting all your experience to the highest advantage to others.

BUCKMINSTER FULLER

GLOWING HEART

The wonderful family is the family that, because it has known security within four walls, has warmed itself at the glowing heart of love and has been renewed by the knowledge that mutual helpfulness can extend this to a troubled and distrustful world.

ELIZABETH YATES

HOMETOWNS

A man may travel far in his life, but there is always a small part of him that never leaves the town where he was born and the neighborhood where he spent his boyhood. Hometowns can be big or small—a hamlet hardly on the highway or the neighborhood of a large city. But large or small, a hometown holds the memories of youth.

DAN VALENTINE

RING AROUND THE WORLD

Ring around the world,
Taking hands together,
All across the temperate
And the torrid weather.

Past the royal palm trees,
By the ocean sand,
Make a ring around the world
Taking each other's hand.

In the valleys, on the hill,
Over the prairie spaces,
There's a ring around the world
Made of children's friendly faces.

ANNETTE WYNNE

We cannot live for ourselves alone. Our lives are connected by a thousand invisible threads, and along these sympathetic fibers, our actions run as causes and return to us as results.

HERMAN MELVILLE

The world moves forward on the feet of little children.

HERBERT HOOVER

News of the Decade

of _____

News Headlines

Popular Songs

Political Figures

Best Movies

Fashions and Fads

Latest Dances

Best-selling Books

Winning Teams

Popular Entertainers

News of the Decade

of _____

News.Headlines

Popular Songs

Political Figures

Best Movies

Fashions and Fads

Latest Dances

Best-selling Books

Winning Teams

Popular Entertainers

Together at Christmas

THE KEEPSAKES OF CHRISTMAS

The souvenirs within the heart
are treasures made of time:
the warmth of logs upon the hearth,
a winter hill to climb;
the glow that shines in children's eyes,
the sunlight on the snow,
the fragrant scent of Christmas cake,
a sleigh ride long ago;
the candles lit to welcome friends,
the snowman on the lawn,
the laughter of a loving voice,
the light of Christmas dawn.

The faith and hope that Christmas brings
will linger, not depart,
for these, the joyous memories,
are saved within the heart.

VIRGINIA COVEY BOSWELL

God bless the master of this house,
  The mistress, also,
And all the little children,
  That round the table go;
And all your kind and kinsmen
  That dwell both far and near;
I wish you a Merry Christmas,
  And a Happy New Year.

OLD ENGLISH CAROL

On the eve of Christmas
In the firelight's glow
Lie all the lovely unsaid things
That old friends know.

CHRISTMAS MAGIC

The joy of brightening other lives, bearing others' burdens, easing others' loads and supplanting empty hearts and lives with generous gifts becomes for us the magic of Christmas.

W. C. JONES

From PICKWICK PAPERS

And numerous indeed are the hearts to which Christmas brings a brief season of happiness and enjoyment. How many families whose members have been dispersed and scattered far and wide in the restless struggles of life are then reunited, and meet once again in that happy state of companionship and mutual good-will which is a source of such pure and unalloyed delight.

Happy, happy Christmas, that can win us back to the delusions of our childish days; that can recall to the old man the pleasures of his youth; that can transport the sailor and the traveller, thousands of miles away, back to his own fireside and his quiet home!

CHARLES DICKENS

THE LITTLE FIRS

The little firs demurely stand
In studious rows, on either hand,
On winter days about like these,
All learning to be Christmas trees.

JOYFUL TIME

The Holiday Season is a special time when families draw together, reaffirming well-loved customs and fundamental beliefs. It is a joyful, eager time for the children, rich with make-believe and laughter—for their elders a time of pride and pleasure, of memories of things past and imagining of things to come. It is a time of gratitude, compassion, hope and faith. Gratitude for the many blessings on this land and for trials withstood. Compassion for the less fortunate. Hope for a better world of peace and justice. Faith in our ability to grow and to build. For our way of life is a good one—strong and free and full of promise—and one in which we may rear our children with confidence.

NEW YORK LIFE INSURANCE COMPANY

Christmas is a gift from God that a man cannot keep until he gives it to someone else.

DOROTHY CAMERON SMITH

CHRISTMAS PAGEANT

Oh, my beloved child
Thank you again for Christmas.
In your eyes I can see
The innocence and the glory of the Christ
    Child.
God's baby Son lives in you,
And His precious gift of hope and eternity
Is your gift to me.

BEVERLY EDELBLUTE

Blessed is the season which engages the whole world in a conspiracy of love.

HAMILTON WRIGHT MABIE

KINDEST TIME

Christmas-time is the best time because it is the kindest time. Nobody ever felt very happy without feeling very kind, and nobody ever felt very kind without feeling at least a little happy. So, of course, either way about the happiest time is the kindest time—that's this time.

BOOTH TARKINGTON

RENDEZVOUS

The old enchantment of my childhood days
Returns to me again on Christmas Eve:
I put aside prosaic grown-up ways
And find a magic world of make-believe.
When all the household lie in quiet sleep
And through the windows starlight softly
    gleams,
I steal away and in the silence keep
A rendezvous with memories and dreams.

I hear the beat of hoofs on crusted snow,
The sound of bells across the starry night,
And briefly glimpse before I turn to go
A flash of scarlet in the eerie light.
Reluctantly, at last, I mount the stairs
And kneel to say my first remembered
    prayers.

EUNICE L. SWALLUM

Christmas is the day that holds all time together.

ALEXANDER SMITH

MERRY CHRISTMAS

Did you ever consider what a friend means by the phrase, "Merry Christmas"? Merry Christmas! What a cheery greeting it is. It brings the full warmth of friendly regard. Forget your troubles and be joyful. There is lots of fun and goodness in life, especially at Christmas. That is what the fine old greeting means. When anyone wishes me a Merry Christmas, it always does me good, for I recall that the Bible says, "A merry heart doeth good like a medicine." So the greeting, "Merry Christmas," is really wishing you happiness, good health, and much joy.

NORMAN VINCENT PEALE

CHRISTMAS BREAD

At Christmastime a neighbor brings us
　　bread,
homemade and plain amid the festival,
a gift that nourishes a deeper need
than fancy for the fantasy of Yule.

The loaf—a shape that's not been
　　redesigned,
firm to the cut, sweet in the crumb.
"To open now and eat" as manna gleaned,
rough-crusted, perishable as any lamb.

We who are close to having everything
take pause and find the richest gift is here,
for in our daily bread and its breaking
we keep the soul of Christmas all the year.

JEAN EVANS

It is good to be children sometimes and never better than at Christmas when its mighty Founder was a child Himself.

CHARLES DICKENS

A SONG IN THE AIR

There's a song in the air!
There's a star in the sky!
There's a mother's deep prayer
And a baby's low cry!
And the star rains its fire while the
　　beautiful sing,
For the manger of Bethlehem cradles a
　　King!

There's a tumult of joy
O'er the wonderful birth,
For the Virgin's sweet boy
Is the Lord of the earth.
Ay! the star rains its fire while the beautiful
　　sing,
For the manger of Bethlehem cradles a
　　King!

We rejoice in the light,
And we echo the song
That comes down thro' the night
From the heavenly throng
Ay! we shout to the lovely evangel they
　　bring,
And we greet in His cradle our Saviour and
　　King!

JOSIAH GILBERT HOLLAND

CHRISTMAS IS SHARING

Christmas is a sharing of joys, memories, homes, and thoughts. A sharing of what we have with our loved ones and with those who are less fortunate.

Christmas is a sharing of emotions; a sharing of our hopes and dreams for the year to come; a sharing of food, conversation, and laughter.

Christmas is a sharing in the beauty and wonder of the little Child who has inspired millions of lives since that night when angels sang, "Glory to God in the Highest!"

PEARL S. BUCK

BELLS, STARLIGHT AND SONG

I will never hear a Christmas song,
Never hear the joyous ring
Of bells but I shall want to bring
(Though gone these many years and long)
All of the homeless, home.

Whenever I see a star burning
Like a flame in the Christmas sky
I turn toward childhood and the dawn
Of other Christmas days—(lest
The blazing fires of late December
Grow cold and I no more remember
Eager footsteps by the door.)

I never see a yule-log glowing
When night comes down without knowing
My heart will soon be going, going
The homing-way once more.

MAY GRAY

Welcome! all Wonders in one sight!
   Eternity shut in a span.
Summer in winter, day in night,
   Heaven in earth, and God in man.
Great little one! whose all-embracing birth
   Lifts earth to heaven, stoops heav'n to
      earth!

RICHARD CRASHAW

What can I give Him
Poor as I am?
If I were a shepherd,
I would give Him a lamb,
If I were a Wise Man,
I would do my part,—
But what can I give Him,
Give my heart.

CHRISTINA ROSETTI

THE CHILDREN'S CHRISTMAS DREAMS

As fragile as an icicle that's wrought by
   winter's cold,
      They are formed in mid-December before
      the season's very old.
Within the minds of children they are born
   and then they grow,
      Each one unique but similar, like falling
      flakes of snow.
They come at you while you hustle
   preparing for The Day,
      But if your heart is not in tune they
      wither and they stray.
So listen to them carefully, then put them
   tenderly aside
      With all the cherished ornaments that
         you so carefully hide.
And sometime on a Christmas when today
   seems long ago
      You'll recall their happy voices and their
      faces all aglow,
Their excitement, the anxiety in spite of all
   their schemes.
      The wonder of their youthful years—the
      children's Christmas dreams.

JANET D. MANCHESTER

TOUCH HANDS

Ah, friends, dear friends, as years go on and
heads get gray, how fast the guests do go!
   Touch hands, touch hands, with those
that stay.
   Strong hands to weak, old hand to young,
around the Christmas board, touch hands.
   The false forget, the foe forgive, for every
guest will go and every fire burn low and
cabin empty stand.
   Forget, forgive, for who may say that
Christmas day may ever come to host or
guest again.

WILLIAM HENRY HARRISON

Photographs

Moments to Remember

JESUS' BIRTHDAY

And did Mary bake a little cake
  When Jesus' birthday came?
Did Joseph carve a wooden toy
  And mark it with his name?
And did his mother make him wait
Till she could set it by his plate,
  And was he happy, just the same
  As you are, on your birthday?
I wish I knew! But long ago
  When Jesus was a boy,
They must have had some loving ways
  Of showing him their joy
When he was eight, and nine, and ten;
It wasn't very different then—
  Families remembered—just the same
  As yours does on your birthday!

                  EDITH KENT BATTLE

From HOLIDAYS

The holiest of all holidays are those
Kept by ourselves in silence and apart;
The secret anniversaries of the heart,
When the full river of feeling overflows.

        HENRY WADSWORTH LONGFELLOW

The family is a storehouse in which the world's finest treasures are kept. Yet the only gold you'll find is golden laughter. The only silver is in the hair of Dad and Mom. The family's only real diamond is on Mother's left hand; yet can it sparkle like children's eyes at Christmas, or shine half as bright as the candles on a birthday cake?

                    ALAN BECK

5TH OF JULY PARADE

She hears drums marching down the street
With Sousa music in their beat;
The slender trombones stepping high,
Are sliding notes into the sky.

She cannot watch parades dry-eyed,
As this one struts in conscious pride
With pie tin drums that come from home,
And tissue paper on a comb!

            RALPH W. SEAGER

ON ANNIVERSARIES

Anniversaries can be hollow affairs, if all they can recount is longevity. How tragic if a backward glance enables us to do nothing but count days. It is possible to accumulate a great score of days with nothing to show for them but a semi-colon. "All the days of Methuselah were 969 years; and he died." Anniversaries provide an occasion to examine the semi-colon in our own life and in the lives of others. We count the value of a life not by the number of its days but by the number and importance of its ideas, its interests, its contributions to others, the goodness it spreads, the love it generates. Anniversaries provide an occasion for examination and resolve. It is a time to become concerned about dimensions of life other than length—concerned about the breadth and depth and height. Anniversaries call us to look at the heights of life. Spirits need to reach for great hopes and great faith. Anniversaries are times of reaching higher.

            W. HEWLETT STITH

BIRTHDAY WISHES

May you have the rare happiness of an undistracted, whole-hearted journey toward a goal you believe is God's plan for your life.

May you be given strength to reject the good while searching for the best.

When you stumble and fall, may you always fall forward, toward your goal.

May you enjoy the richness of soul that is the result of seeing that your spiritual income always exceeds your expenditures.

May you enjoy the exciting fun of keeping company with the great and riding on the shoulders of giants.

May you read the best, thus spending hours with the towering souls of all ages.

As a tree continues to grow to its dying day, may you grow in wisdom and spirit as long as you live.

May you always possess your possessions; may they never possess you.

May you always have the wisdom and strength to say "No" to some things so that you can say "Yes" to other important things.

May you know the joys of fellowship with those you love, who return your love, and with those who love the things you love, to whom you look with admiration and trust and with whom you look toward the same purposes and goals. May you know the happiness that multiplies as you divide it with others.

May you be blessed with health and with the laughter that is God's good medicine for all men.

May you have the steadying confidence that when you have, by God's grace, done the best that is in you, you can leave the rest to Him, and to time, to determine its value.

May you find the changeless, steady values in a changeful and unsteady world, and the Eternal amidst matters that erode and vanish.

May you be blessed with a memory that is both splendid and poor; splendid in its remembrance of kindnesses you have received from God and man, and often forgetful of the benefits you have conferred on others.

May life not be too stormy, yet may you have enough clouds in your sky to make breathtaking dawns and beautiful sunsets.

May you have the joyful satisfaction of making a difference for good wherever you go.

HAROLD E. KOHN

From THANKSGIVING DAY

Over the river and through the wood,
    To grandfather's house we go;
        The horse knows the way
        To carry the sleigh
    Through the white and drifted snow.

Over the river and through the wood—
    Oh, how the wind does blow!
        It stings the toes
        And bites the nose,
    As over the ground we go.

Over the river and through the wood,
    Trot fast, my dapple-gray!
        Spring over the ground,
        Like a hunting hound!
    For this is Thanksgiving Day.

LYDIA MARIA CHILD

201

Family Anniversaries

occasion ———————————————— date ——————————

occasion ———————————————— date ——————————

occasion ———————————————— date ——————————

occasion ———————————————— date ——————————

occasion ———————————————— date ——————————

occasion ———————————————— date ——————————

occasion ———————————————— date ——————————

occasion ———————————————— date ——————————

occasion ———————————————— date ——————————

occasion ———————————————— date ——————————

occasion ———————————————— date ——————————

Photographs

Grandmother's House

WHAT IS A GRANDMOTHER?

A grandmother is a lady who has no children of her own. She likes other people's little girls and boys. A grandfather is a man grandmother. He goes for walks with the boys, and they talk about fishing and stuff like that.

Grandmothers don't have to do anything except to be there. They're old so they shouldn't play hard or run. It is enough if they drive us to the market where the pretend horse is, and have a lot of dimes ready. Or if they take us for walks, they should slow down past things like pretty leaves and caterpillars. They should never say, "Hurry up."

Usually grandmothers are fat, but not too fat to tie your shoes. They wear glasses and funny underwear. They can take their teeth and gums off.

Grandmothers don't have to be smart, only answer questions like, "Why isn't God married?" and "How come dogs chase cats?"

Grandmothers don't talk baby talk like visitors do, because it is hard to understand. When they read to us they don't skip, or mind if it is the same story over again.

Everybody should try to have a grandmother, especially if you don't have television, because they are the only grown-ups who have time.

A THIRD GRADE GIRL

By the time the youngest children have learned to keep the house tidy, the oldest grandchildren are on hand to tear it to pieces again.

CHRISTOPHER MORLEY

GRANDFATHER'S CANE

Grandfather's cane does wonderful things:
It tips up a stone so I, by peeping,
Can see crawly worms and little bugs
    creeping;
It stirs up the leaves to show me a cricket,
Or the beautiful world of a bud in a thicket;
Then raising much higher than I can reach,
It hooks down the biggest, the yellowest
    peach.

Grandfather's cane knows how to have fun;
It bucks like a bronco and tries to unseat
    me,
Or plays tic-tac-toe yet won't always beat
    me
And when I am tired and my feet begin
    slowing,
Hitched into my belt it gives me a towing.
Sometimes I'm a bear and get caught in its
    trap,
Yet it cuddles beside me when I take a nap.
It's hard to explain a stick with a brain,
But this one is different—it's Grandfather's
    cane!

RALPH W. SEAGER

He is a wise man who chooses a good grandfather.

OLIVER WENDELL HOLMES

206

GRANDSONS

How easily they step
into the skies!
These sapling youths
whose roots we are.
We stand—they wave—
curtailing their good-byes
to seek new truths
behind a star.

JANET MORGAN

AGE IS OPPORTUNITY

For age is opportunity no less
Than youth itself, though in another dress;
And as the evening twilight fades away,
The sky is filled with stars, invisible by day.

HENRY WADSWORTH LONGFELLOW

A LOVELY SURPRISE

Life has started all over for me,
The young years of happiness
Have come again in a sweeter form
Than a mother could ever guess.
The love and devotion I gave my child
I thought I could give no other,
But life held a lovely surprise for me—
This year I became a grandmother.

KAY ANDREW

FAMILY PORTRAIT

A floral hat of blue and white . . .
Mother wore to church tonight.
Shy Aunt Bessie preferred gray,
The color of a rainy day.

A plain black hat seemed more sedate . . .
To stern, staunch, steady sister Kate.

But Grandma chose a hat of red
And placed it proudly on her head . . .
A badge for all her friends to see—
Grandma's independency.

JUNE WEAVER

IN GRANDMOTHER'S CORNER

In grandmother's corner the sunshine stays
  Golden and bright in the gloomiest days.
In grandmother's sweet benignant face
  There's a lightsome look for the loneliest
    place.
And I think the flowers are glad to bloom
  In one dear little window of
    grandmother's room.

MARGARET E. SANGSTER

From Generation to Generation

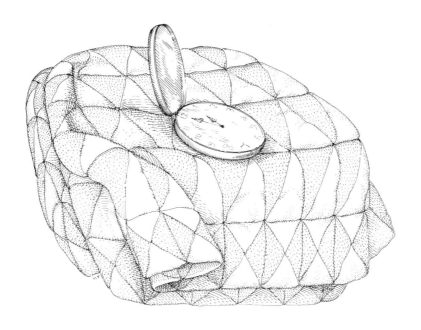

I love old things:
Weather-beaten, worn things,
Cracked, broken, torn things,
The old sun, the old moon,
The old earth's face,
Old wine in dim flagons,
Old ships and old wagons—
Old coin and old lace,
Rare old lace.

WILSON MacDONALD

REFLECTIONS AT EIGHTY

I am most of all thankful for my birthplace
and early nurture in the warm atmosphere
of a spiritually-minded home, with a mani-
fest touch of saintliness in it; thankful indeed that from the cradle I was saturated
with the Bible and immersed in an environment of religion of experience and reality. It
was a peculiar grace that I was born into
that great inheritance of spiritual wisdom
and faith, accumulated through generations of devotion and sacrificial love. I
never can be grateful enough for what was
done for me by my progenitors before I
came on the scene. They produced the spiritual atmosphere of my youth. I became heir
of a vast invisible inheritance, more important in my life than ancestral lands or
chests full of the gold of Ophir. There is
nothing I would exchange for that.

RUFUS M. JONES

CONTINUITY

If a thing is old, it is a sign that it was fit to
live. Old families, old customs, old styles
survive because they are fit to survive. The
guarantee of continuity is quality.

EDDIE RICKENBACKER

ONE STEP AT A TIME

One step at a time, and that well placed,
    We reach the grandest height;
One stroke at a time, earth's hidden stores
    Will slowly come to light;
One seed at a time, and the forest grows;
One drop at a time, and the river flows
    Into the boundless sea.

One word at a time, and the greatest book
    Is written and is read;
One stone at a time, and a palace rears
    Aloft its stately head;
One blow at a time, and the tree's cleft
        through,
And a city will stand where the forest grew
    A few short years before.

One grain of knowledge, and that well
        stored,
    Another and more on them;
As time rolls on your mind will shine
    With many a garnered gem
Of thought and wisdom. And time will tell
"One thing at a time, and that done well,"
    Is wisdom's proven rule.

IMMORTAL MINDS

If we work upon marble, it will perish. If we
work upon brass, time will efface it. If we
rear temples, they will crumble to dust. But
if we work upon men's immortal minds, if
we imbue them with high principles, with
just fear of God and love of their fellow
man, we engrave on those tablets something which no time can efface, and which
will brighten and brighten to all eternity.

DANIEL WEBSTER

From THE WILL OF THE LATE GEORGE LOUNSBURY OF LONDON

I give good fathers and mothers, in trust for their children, all good little words of praise and encouragement, and all quaint pet names and endearments; and I charge said parents to use them justly, but generously, as the needs of their children shall require.

I leave the children inclusively, but only for the term of their childhood, the flowers of the fields and the blossoms of the woods, and the right to play among them freely, according to the custom of children, warning them, at the same time, against the thistle and the thorns. And I devise to the children the banks of the brooks and the golden sands beneath the water thereof, and the odors of the willow that dip therein, and the white clouds that float high over the giant trees. And I leave to the children the long, long days to be merry in a thousand ways, and the night and the moon, and the train of the Milky Way to wonder at, but subject, nevertheless, to the rights hereinafter given to lovers.

I devise to boys, jointly, all the idle fields and commons, where ball may be played, all pleasant waters where one may swim, all snow-clad hills where one may fish, or where, when grim winter comes, one may skate, to have and to hold the same for the period of their boyhood. And I give to said boys each his own place at the fireside at night with all the pictures that may be seen in the burning wood, to enjoy without hindrance and without any encumbrance of care.

INEXHAUSTIBLE LOVE

All the paternal love which has come down from generation to generation through the channel of human hearts, all the springs of tenderness which have opened in the souls of men, are but as a tiny rill to the boundless ocean when compared with the infinite, exhaustless love of God. Tongue cannot utter it; pen cannot portray it. You may meditate upon it every day of your life; you may search the Scriptures diligently in order to understand it; you may summon every power and capability that God has given you, in an endeavor to comprehend the love and compassion of the Heavenly Father; and yet there is infinity beyond.

ELLEN G. WHITE

SAINTS WITHOUT HALOS

The sainthoods of the fireside and of the marketplace—they wear no glory round their heads. They do their duties in the strength of God; they have their martyrdoms and win their palms; they leave a benediction and a force behind them on the earth when they go up to heaven.

PHILLIPS BROOKS

We should so live and labor in our time that that which came to us as seed may go to the next generation as blossom, and that which comes to us as blossoms may go to them as fruit.

HENRY WARD BEECHER

Every man is an omnibus in which all of his ancestors are seated.

OLIVER WENDELL HOLMES

Important Family Events

event _____

_____

_____ date _____

event _____

_____

_____ date _____

event _____

_____

_____ date _____

event _____

_____

_____ date _____

Photographs

Photographs

Years of Gold

HONEST, WOULDN'T YOU?

Did you ever think you'd like to
 Back up just a little ways,
And enjoy again the pleasures
 Of your happy boyhood days?

Would you trade your patent leathers
 And your made-to-order clothes
For an hour of runnin' barefoot,
 Squeezin' mud between your toes?

How'd you swap your old dyspepsia
 And your job of findin' fault
For a hatful of green apples
 And a pocketful of salt?

Would you give your fancy tackle
 For a nice long willow pole,
An old can full of fishworms
 And a little sunfish hole?

Oh! we knew you'd say you wouldn't,
 But we're all just grown-up boys,
And it's only pride that robs us
 Of the fun the kid enjoys.

AS I GROW OLD

God keep my heart attuned to laughter
 When youth is done;
When all the days are gray days, coming
 after
 The warmth, the sun.
God keep me then from bitterness, from
 grieving,
 When life seems cold;
God keep me always loving and believing
 As I grow old.

From ULYSSES

Come, my friends.
'Tis not too late to seek a newer world.
Push off, and sitting well in order smite
The sounding furrows; for my purpose
 holds
To sail beyond the sunset, and the baths
Of all the western stars, until I die.
It may be that the gulfs will wash us down;
It may be we shall touch the Happy Isles,
And see the great Achilles, whom we knew.
Tho' much is taken, much abides; and tho'
We are not now that strength which in old
 days
Moved earth and heaven, that which we
 are, we are,—
One equal temper of heroic hearts,
Made weak by time and fate, but strong in
 will
To strive, to seek, to find, and not to yield.
              ALFRED LORD TENNYSON

I'm old enough to feel an occasional twist of
muscle but young enough to tap my toes at
the first sound of music.

I'm old enough to accept life's twists and
turns but young enough to challenge apa-
thy or defeat.

I'm old enough to cherish memories yet
young enough to promote new experiences.

I'm old enough to value tradition yet
young enough to sponsor change.

I'm old enough to savor quiet hours yet
young enough to seek laughter and joy.

I'm old enough to have a few regrets but
young enough to use them as stepping
stones toward progress.

I'm old enough to respect the accomplishment of science yet young enough to accept
the simplicity of God.

              BASILLA E. NEILAN

We have lived and loved together
  Through many changing years;
We have shared each other's gladness
  And wept each other's tears;
I have known ne'er a sorrow
  That was long unsoothed by thee;
For thy smiles can make a summer
  Where darkness else would be.

CHARLES JEFFERYS

ON GROWING OLD

An apple's the fruition of a springtime's
  bursting bloom.
The timber from some leaf-draped tree will
  serve to make a room.
The seasons are but facets on the diamond
  of our days.
And each reflects in different form the
  beauty of life's rays.
I have known the joys of youth. To me
  they'll never hold
a candle to the warming thrill of gently
  growing old;
of basking in the silvery glow of age's
  ripening rays
and watching dim tomorrows change to
  hallowed yesterdays.

DWAYNE LAWS

AS I GROW OLD

Grant me, Lord, your richest gift
Sound health of mind and body
Absorbing hobbies and friends to share
  them—
So I can approach my autumn
with anticipation
rather than wistful memories.

HYACINTH RIZZO

FACES

I know not which I like the best
  The face of youth or age;
I've seen fair pictures of them both
  Upon life's pleasing page.
No doubt the smiles of youth we'd keep
  Did we possess the art,
But wrinkles on the face are sweet
  When dimples dot the heart.

RUTH NEAL

HAPPIEST SEASON

When spring comes and in the soft air the buds are breaking on the trees and they are covered with blossoms, I think "How beautiful is spring!" And when the summer comes and covers the trees with its heavy foliage and singing birds are among the branches, I think "How beautiful is summer!" When autumn loads them with golden fruit and their leaves bear the gorgeous tint of frost, I think, "How beautiful is autumn!" And when it is winter and there is neither foliage nor fruit, then I look up through the leafless branches, as I never could until now, and see stars shine.

"I never ask advice about growing,"
Alice said indignantly.
  "Too proud?" Humpty Dumpty inquired.
  Alice felt even more indignant
at this suggestion. "I mean," she said,
"that one cannot help growing old."
  "One can't, perhaps," said Humpty
Dumpty, "but two can."

LEWIS CARROLL

BEATITUDES FOR FRIENDS
OF THE AGED

Blessed are they who understand
  My faltering step and palsied hand.
Blessed are they who know my ears today
  Must strain to catch the things they say.
Blessed are they who seem to know
  That my eyes are dim and my wits are
    slow.
Blessed are they who looked away
  When my coffee was spilled at the table
    today.
Blessed are they with a cheery smile
  Who stop to chat for a little while.
Blessed are they who never say,
  "You've told that story twice today."
Blessed are they who know the ways
  To bring back memories of yesterdays.
Blessed are they who make it known that
    I'm loved,
  Respected and not alone.
Blessed are they who ease the days
  On my journey Home in loving ways.

ESTER MAY WALKER

RESPONSIBILITY

Marriages may be made in heaven, but man
is responsible for the maintenance work.

OLD CLOCK

Old clock, you hurry me all day
While you, unhurried tick away.
Your hands just point to state the hour
While my hands cook and clean and scour.
I run to tasks both great and small
Then listen while I hear you call.
I need more time and hope to borrow.
You calmly say, "There's still tomorrow."

DOROTHY L. CAMPBELL

BREAD

Some labor gathers to itself a light;
This I have found where women making
    bread
Perform anew an ancient, simple rite,
That men and little children might be fed.
Something about the handling of white
    flour
Is beautiful: the thought of sun on wheat;
The shining silver of a quick, late shower,
A great mill glimmering through the
    harvest heat.

And old as life, a fadeless picture still,
The gold of grain crushed fine beneath a
    stone;
Two women grinding at an ancient mill,
And one is taken, one is left alone,
O, always, somewhere, women have made
    bread,
That men and little children might be fed.

GRACE NOLL CROWELL

The evening of a well-spent life brings its
lamp with it.

JOSEPH JOUBERT

For she is wise, if I can judge of her,
And fair she is, if that mine eyes be true,
And true she is, as she hath prov'd herself;
And therefore, like herself, wise, fair, and
    true,
Shall she be placed in my constant soul.

WILLIAM SHAKESPEARE

A kind old age means growing old on the
outside without growing old inside.

DOM HELDER CAMARA

WHEN I GROW OLD

These are the pleasures I would hold
As life's day wanes to sunset gold,
And neighbors whisper I am old:

A little house, not hard to keep,
Over whose roof the quiet days creep,
With time for thought and prayer and
    sleep.

A little garden, glimmering near,
Where old-time blossoms quaint and dear,
Unfold in beauty year by year.

A little work to do with zest,
Making life easier and more blest
For household mates whom I love best.

A little group of long-tried friends,
Whose presence joy and comfort lends
Until the final peace descends.

These are the pleasures I would hold,
As life's day wanes to sunset gold.
And neighbors whisper I am old.

EFFIE SMITH ELY

Autumn is the mellower season, and what
we lose in flowers we more than gain in
fruits.

SAMUEL BUTLER

The goal in marriage is not to think alike,
but to think together.

ROBERT C. DODDS

You cannot control the length of your life,
but you can control its width and depth.

DAVID S. SCHULLER

At sunrise every soul is born again.

WALTER MALONE

PRAYER

O God, our Heavenly Father, whose gift is
length of days, help us to make the noblest
use of mind and body in our advancing
years. According to our strength, apportion
Thou our work. As Thou hast pardoned our
transgressions, so sift the ingatherings of
our memory, that evil may grow dim, and
good may shine forth clearly.

We thank Thee for Thy gifts, and especially for Thy presence and the love of friends
in heaven and on earth. Grant us new ties of
friendship, new opportunities for service,
joy in the growth and happiness of children, and sympathy with those who bear the
burdens of the world, clear thought and
quiet faith.

Teach us to bear infirmities with cheerful
patience. Keep us from narrow pride in out-
grown ways, blind eyes that will not see the
good of change, impatient judgments of
methods and experiments of others.

Let Thy peace fuel our spirits through all
the trials of our waning powers. Take from
us all fear of death and all despair or undue
love of life, so that, with glad hearts at rest
in Thee, we may await the time when Thou
shalt call us home.

LENA SORABJI

Never have I enjoyed youth so thoroughly
as I have in my old age.

GEORGE SANTAYANA

Lingering Memories

From MY LOST YOUTH

Often I think of the beautiful town
  That is seated by the sea;
Often in thought go up and down
The pleasant streets of that dear old town,
  And my youth comes back to me.
    And a verse of a Lapland song
    Is haunting my memory still:
    "A boy's will is the wind's will,
And the thoughts of youth are long, long
    thoughts."
      HENRY WADSWORTH LONGFELLOW

Pleasant memories are private treasures
that moths cannot corrupt nor thieves
break in and steal.

      JOHN KIERAN

Those years lie in memory like a handful of
jewels that sparkle as I turn them over.
Why do past years sparkle so? They were
full of ordinary things while they were
being lived; they were often dusty and dull;
but they are jewels now, many-colored, various, lighted with lights that time cannot
dim nor tears drown.

      AMY CARMICHAEL

'Mid pleasures and palaces though we may
  roam,
Be it ever so humble, there's no place like
  home;
A charm from the skies seems to hallow us
  there,
Which, seek thro' the world, is ne'er met
  with elsewhere.

      J. H. PAYNE

The happiest moments of my life have been
the few which I have passed at home in the
bosom of my family. Abstracted from home,
I know no happiness in this world.

      THOMAS JEFFERSON

BAREFOOT

And we went barefoot through the dewy
  grass,
Wishing that our summertime would never
  pass
Where lovely leisure laughed beneath green
  trees,
And sorrow only came from skinned-up
  knees.
Sometimes fishing poles, sometimes wild
  flowers
Lured us through the woods—enchanted
  hours
Filled an imagination drawn from fairy
  tales—
We swaggered over burning decks or set
  our sails
For castle turrets somewhere in the sky;
We dreamed our rainbow dreams on clouds
  piled high.
So shall we barefoot go across life's sands
To search for our own lost childhood lands.

      NAOMI HOLT BARNARD

A MOTHER'S PRAYER

Give me patience when little hands
Tug at me with ceaseless small demands.
Give me gentle words and smiling eyes,
And keep my lips from hasty, sharp replies.
Let me not in weariness, confusion, or noise
Obscure my vision from life's fleeting joys
That when in years to come my house is
  still
Beautiful memories its rooms may fill.

A mother's love is the golden link that binds youth to age; and he is still but a child, however time may have furrowed his cheek or silvered his brow, who can yet recall, with a softened heart, the fond devotion or the gentle chidings of the best friend that God ever gives us.

CHRISTIAN NESTELL BOVEE

From DAILY BREAD

Oh, I am rich in treasures stored away—
Old ecstasies and half-remembered joys;
Prismatic dawns that faded to white noons;
Knowledge forgotten; songs my mother
    sang;
The scent of flowers that withered long ago;
Wounds that have healed and left but little
    scars
To show where once the very lifeblood
    ebbed;
Sorrows that long since lost their bitterness
And only knit me closer to my kind;
Music that lingers though its notes are
    stilled;
Voices and hands and lips that I have loved.

WINFRED ERNEST GARRISON

SOMETIMES

Across the fields of yesterday
    He sometimes comes to me,
A little lad just back from play—
    The lad I used to be.

And yet he smiles so wistfully
    Once he has crept within,
I wonder if he hopes to see
    The man I might have been.

THOMAS S. JONES, JR.

From IN THE GOOD OLD SUMMER TIME

To swim in the pool, you'd play 'hookey'
    from school,
Good old summer time;
You'd play "ring-a-rosie" with Jim, Kate
    and Josie,
Good old summer time,
Those days full of pleasure we now fondly
    treasure,
When we never thought it a crime,
To go stealing cherries, with faces brown as
    berries,
Good old summer time.

REN SHIELDS

GRATITUDE

For sunlit hours and visions clear,
For all remembered faces dear,
For comrades of a single day,
Who sent us stronger on our way,
For friends who shared the year's long road,
And bore with us the common load,
For hours that levied heavy tolls,
But brought us nearer to our goals,
For insights won through toil and tears,
We thank the Keeper of our years.

CLYDE McGEE

I WENT TO SCHOOL WITH HIM

Some friends are different from the rest,
A glance, a smile, we know
We have a rendezvous with youth
That comes from long ago.
Sometimes upon a crowded street,
Or in a church, where lights are dim,
I see a face that warms my heart—
I went to school with him.

ETHEL HOPPER

Home Eternal

THE RAINBOW

It cannot be that the earth is man's only abiding place. It cannot be that life is a mere bubble, cast up by eternity to float a moment on its waves and then sink into nothingness. Else why is it that the glorious aspirations, which leap like angels from the temple of our hearts, are forever wandering unsatisfied? Why is it that all stars that hold their festival around the midnight throne are set above the grasp of our limited faculties, forever mocking us with their unapproachable glory?

And why is it that bright forms of human beauty, presented to our view, are taken from us, leaving the thousand streams of our affections to flow back in Alpine torrents upon our hearts?

There is a realm where the rainbow never fades, where the stars will be spread out before us like islands that slumber in the ocean, and where the beautiful that now passes before us like a shadow will stay in our presence forever.

GEORGE D. PRENTICE

I hold it true, whate'er befall
I feel it, when I sorrow most
'Tis better to have loved and lost
Than never to have loved at all.

ALFRED LORD TENNYSON

HOME

Our earthly homes are simple things
    Of plaster and of board,
Sometimes as humble as the nest
    Built by the wildwood bird.
And yet, through all our lives, our hearts
    Cling to this childhood home
Of hallowed, precious memories,
    No matter where we roam.
And so I often think about
    How dear, how very dear,
Our heavenly home will come to be
    With every passing year.
That home where we shall meet and dwell
    With loved ones gone before,
And sometimes, looking up, shall see
    Our Lord come through the door.
Sweet home, where all our fulfilled joys
    Become rich memories,
And ever deeper pleasures crowd
    The long eternities!

MARTHA SNELL NICHOLSON

Life is the childhood of immortality.

DANIEL A. POLING

NATURE

As a fond mother, when the day is o'er,
  Leads by the hand her little child to bed,
  Half willing, half reluctant to be led
  And leave his broken playthings on the
    floor,
Still gazing at them through the open door,
  Nor wholly reassured and comforted
  By promises of others in their stead,
  Which, though more splendid, may not
    please him more;
So Nature deals with us, and takes away
  Our playthings one by one, and by the
    hand
  Leads us to rest so gently, that we go
Scarce knowing if we wish to go or stay,
  Being too full of sleep to understand
  How far the unknown transcends the
    what we know.

      HENRY WADSWORTH LONGFELLOW

Those who live in the Lord never see each
other for the last time.

      GERMAN PROVERB

SO THE GOOD DIE YOUNG

She never said anything to make us stare.
But she lived her life with a certain air
Of knowing what the sun intends to do
With curly clouds, and why the blue
Of the ancient sky is always new.
She listened to people—and their words
    grew wise
Because of the wisdom within her eyes.
Lightly as leaves cling, the quick years
    clung
About her shoulders till her songs were
    sung.
Then she, at ninety, being good, died young.

      BONARO W. OVERSTREET

How rich this earth seems when we regard
it—crowded with the loves of home! Yet I
am now getting to go home—to leave this
world of homes and go home. When I reach
that home, shall I even then seek yet to go
home? Even then, I believe, I shall seek a
yet warmer, deeper, purer home in the
deeper knowledge of God—in the truer love
of my fellow men. Eternity will be—my
heart and my faith tell me—a traveling
homeward, but in jubilation and confidence
and vision of the beloved.

      GEORGE MacDONALD

THE HILLS OF HOME

The hills of home—what magic words!
My thoughts fly out like fleet-winged birds
To where those hills and valleys lie
Beneath the clouds in God's great sky.

The hills of home, where life was new
And filled with zest to see and do;
Untrammeled joys of childhood's play
Made full the hours of each new day.

The hills of home, where I have known
Life's changing moods; the winds have
    blown
Both good and ill. The joys, the tears,
Have made the harvest of the years.

The hills of home—how blue the sky!
How fair the fields in memory's eye!
How dear the ones that we have known
Who walked with us the hills of home!

The hills of home—by faith I see
Them stretching through eternity.
Unwearied there my feet shall be,
Undimmed my eye when I shall see
The hills of home!

MARJORIE STODOLA

MY EARTHLY WORK

Lord, let me not die until I've done for Thee
My earthly work, whatever it may be.
Call me not hence with mission unfulfilled;
Let me not leave my space of ground
    untilled;
Impress this truth upon me that not one
Can do my portion that I leave undone.

LIVING WELL

He liveth long who liveth well;
    All else is being flung away;
He liveth longest who can tell
    Of true things truly done each day.

Fill up each hour with what will last;
    Use well the moments as they go;
The life above, when this is past,
    Is ripe fruit of life below.

HORATIUS BONAR

ACKNOWLEDGMENTS

(See additional acknowledgments on p. vi)

E. P. DUTTON, COMPANY, INC.: An excerpt from *Three to Get Married* by Fulton J. Sheen. Copyright 1951 by Appleton-Century-Crofts; excerpts from *No Mean City* by Simeon Strunsky. Copyright, 1944 by E. P. Dutton, Company, Inc.; "Good Night" from *The Susianna Winkle Book* by Dorothy Mason Pierce. Copyright, 1935 by E. P. Dutton, Company, Inc. Renewal 1963 by Dorothy Mason Pierce; an excerpt from "Us Two" from *Now We Are Six* by A. A. Milne. Copyright, 1927 by E. P. Dutton, Company, Inc. Renewal 1955 by A. A. Milne. Also permission of McClelland & Stewart, Toronto, and Metheun Books, London; an excerpt from *Bow Down in Jericho* by Byron Herbert Reece. Copyright, 1950 by Byron Herbert Reece. Renewal 1978 by Eva Mae Reece; an excerpt from *Parents on Trial: Why Kids Go Wrong or Right* by David Wilkerson. Copyright © 1967 by E. P. Dutton, Company, Inc. (A Hawthorne Book).

EDWARD B. MARKS MUSIC CORPORATION: An excerpt from "In the Good Old Summer Time." Copyright by Edward B. Marks Music Corporation.

FOUNDATION FOR CHRISTIAN LIVING: Excerpts from the writings of Norman Vincent Peale.

GIRARD BANK TRUSTEE: "Reflections at Eighty" from the writings of Rufus M. Jones.

GOLDEN QUILL PRESS: "Grandsons" from *Take with You Words* by Janet Morgan. Copyright © 1975 by Golden Quill Press.

HALLMARK GREETING CARDS: "Motherhood" from *The Gypsy Heart* by Emily Carey Alleman. Copyright © 1957.

HAROLD MATSON CO., INC.: An excerpt from *Our Miss Boo* by Margaret Lee Runbeck. Copyright 1942 by Margaret Lee Runbeck. Renewal 1969 by Jessadee R. Scallan. Published by Appleton-Century-Crofts (E. P. Dutton, Co., Inc.).

HARPER & ROW, PUBLISHERS, INC.: From *Poems of Inspiration and Courage* by Grace Noll Crowell: "So Long as There Are Homes" copyright 1936 by Harper & Row, Publishers, Inc. Renewed 1964 by Grace Noll Crowell, "Bread" copyright 1946 by Grace Noll Crowell, "The Bride" copyright 1940 by Harper & Row, Publishers, Inc. Renewed 1968 by Grace Noll Crowell, "Definition" copyright 1936 by Harper & Row, Publishers, Inc. Renewed 1964 by Grace Noll Crowell; Specific excerpt from p. 45 in *The Sense of Wonder* by Rachel Carson. Copyright © by Rachel L. Carson; "The Common Tasks" from *Songs of Hope* by Grace Noll Crowell. Copyright 1938 by Harper & Row, Publishers, Inc. Renewed 1966 by Grace Noll Crowell; "Hug O' War" from *Where the Sidewalk Ends* by Shel Silverstein. Copyright © 1974 by Shel Silverstein; "Animal Crackers" and "Song for a Little House" from *Songs for a Little House* by Christopher Morley. Copyright 1917, 1945 by Christopher Morley; "Ring Around the House" from *All Through the Year* by Annette Wynne (J. B. Lippincott). Copyright 1932, 1960 by Annette Wynne; "Boys' Names" and "Girls' Names" from *Eleanor Farjeon's Poems for Children* by Eleanor Farjeon (J. B. Lippincott). Copyright 1933, 1961 by Eleanor Farjeon. Also by permission of Harold Ober Associates Incorporated; an excerpt from *The Web and the Rock* by Thomas Wolfe. Copyright 1939 by Harper & Row, Publishers, Inc.; excerpts from *Two Together* by Robert C. Dodds. Copyright © 1959, 1962 by Harper & Row, Publishers, Inc.; an excerpt from *Early Autumn* by Louis Bromfield.

Copyright 1925 by Harper & Row, Publishers, Inc.; an excerpt from *The Search for Common Ground* by Howard Thurman. Copyright © 1971 by Harper & Row, Publishers, Inc.; and "Grace at Evening" from *Over the Sea, The Sky* by Edwin McNeill Poteat. Copyright 1945 by Harper & Row, Publishers, Inc.; an excerpt from *The Purpose of the Church and Its Ministry* by H. Richard Niebuhr, p. 35. Copyright © 1956 by Harper & Row, Publishers, Inc.; an excerpt from *Surprised by Light* by Ulrich Schaffer, p. 27. Copyright © 1980 by Ulrich Schaffer.

THE HERBERT HOOVER FOUNDATION: "To Go Fishing," "To Help Us Stay Young," "Bill of Rights," and other excerpts from *Addresses on the American Road, Vols. I–VIII* by Herbert Hoover. Copyrights Vol. I 1938, Vol. II 1940 and Vol. III 1941 by Charles Scribner's Sons; Vol. IV 1946 and Vol. V 1949 by D. Van Nostrand Company; Vol VI 1951, Vol VII © 1955 by Stanford University Press; and Vol. VIII © 1961 by Caxton, Calwell, Idaho.

HOLT, RINEHART AND WINSTON: An excerpt from "A Shropshire Lad"—Authorised Edition—from *The Collected Poems of A. E. Housman* by A. E. Housman. Copyright 1939, 1940, © 1965 by Holt, Rinehart and Winston. Copyright © 1967, 1968 by Robert E. Symons. Also reprinted with the permission of The Society of Authors as the literary representatives of the Estate of A. E. Housman, and Jonathan Cape Ltd., publishers of A. E. Housman's *Collected Poems*; "A Steeple on the House" from *The Poetry of Robert Frost* edited by Edward Connery Lathem. Copyright 1947, © 1969 by Holt, Rinehart and Winston. Copyright © 1975 by Leslie Frost Ballentine.

LESCHER AND LESCHER, LTD.: Excerpts by Clifton Fadiman, first published in *The New Yorker* magazine. Reprinted by permission of Lescher and Lescher, Ltd., on behalf of Clifton Fadiman.

MacARTHUR MEMORIAL FOUNDATION: "Prayer for a Son" by Douglas MacArthur.

MACMILLAN PUBLISHING COMPANY, INC.: An excerpt from *A Faith to Affirm* by James Gordon Gilkey. Copyright 1940 by Macmillan Publishing Co., Inc. Renewed 1968 by Calma H. Gilkey; "Doorbells" from *Poems* by Rachel Field. Copyright © 1957 by Macmillan Publishing Co., Inc.; an excerpt from *The Use of Life* by John Lubbock. Copyright 1894 by Macmillan Publishing Co., Inc.; an excerpt from *Five Bushel Farm* by Elizabeth Coatsworth. Copyright 1939 by Macmillan Publishing Company, Inc. Renewed 1967 by Elizabeth Coatsworth Beston.

MOODY BIBLE INSTITUTE OF CHICAGO: "Christmas Lullaby" and "Prayer at Bedtime" from *He Came with Music* by Helen Frazee-Bower. Copyright © 1963 by The Moody Bible Institute of Chicago. Also reprinted with permission of the Bower Estate; "Home" from *Her Lamp of Faith* by Martha Snell Nicholson. Copyright © 1968 by the Moody Bible Institute of Chicago.

NEW DIRECTIONS PUBLISHING CORPORATION: An excerpt from *New Seeds of Contemplation* by Thomas Merton. Copyright © 1961 by The Abbey of Gethsemani, Inc.

NEW YORK LIFE INSURANCE COMPANY: "A Christmas Prayer."

UNITED METHODIST PUBLISHING HOUSE: "First Good-bye" by Madeleine Laeufer from *Together* magazine, August-September 1972. Copyright © 1972 by The United Methodist Publishing House.

U.S. CATHOLIC: An excerpt from "The Search for Intimacy," an interview with Rev. Dr. Henri J. M. Nouwen by Edward Wakin in *U.S. Catholic* magazine.

Special appreciation is due the following authors or their representatives for permission to include portions of their work:

IOLA M. ANDERSON for "Motherhood."

RICHARD ARMOUR for "Losing Battle" and "Teamwork" from *My Life with Women* by Richard Armour. Copyright © 1968 by Richard Armour, published by McGraw-Hill, Inc.

JAMES ASHLEY for "Graduation" by Nova Trimble Ashley.

GEORGE S. BENSON for an excerpt from his writings.

RABBI BEN ZION BOKSER for an excerpt from "Old Blankets" in *Gifts of Life And Love* by Rabbi Ben Zion Bokser. Copyright © 1975 by Rabbi Ben Zion Bokser, pp. 75–76. Published by Hebrew Publishing Company.

BOY SCOUTS OF AMERICA for "Scouting" by Walter Mac-Peek.

ESTELLE D. BROADRICK for "The Old Home."

THE ESTATE OF RUTH MCAFEE BROWN for an excerpt from the writings of Ruth McAfee Brown.

RICHARD E. BYRD III for an excerpt from *Alone* by Richard E. Byrd. Copyright 1938 by Putnams and Coward McCann.

MARCHETTE CHUTE for "My Dog" reprinted from *Around and About* by Marchette Chute. Copyright © 1957 by E. P. Dutton, Co., Inc.; and "Books Are The Opening of Windows" by Marchette Chute. Originally published in The Wilson Library Bulletin, Feb. 1957, pg. 446.

ESTATE OF ROBERT P. TRISTRAM COFFIN for "The Family Stairs" from *Collected Poems of Robert P. Tristram Coffin* by Robert P. Tristram Coffin. Copyright 1945, 1948 by Robert P. Tristram Coffin. Published by Macmillan Publishing Co., Inc.

THE EXECUTORS OF THE LATE SIR HUGH WALPOLE for an excerpt from *The Silver Thorn, A Book of Stories* by Sir Hugh Walpole. Published by Doubleday & Company, Inc., 1928.

DR. DOROTHY FOSDICK AND ELINOR FOSDICK DOWNS for excerpts from the writings of Harry Emerson Fosdick.

SARA HENDERSON HAY for "After the Crucifixion."

W. S. HYLAND AND THE ESTATE OF WILLIAM L. STIDGER for excerpts from the writings of William L. Stidger.

RUBY A. JONES for "Tribute to a Foster Father."

EDNA MILLS KILEY for "A Little Tree" from *Wildlife on the Rockies* by Enos A. Mills. Copyright 1909 by Enos A. Mills (Houghton Mifflin Co.), 1936, © 1962.

MRS. HAROLD E. KOHN for "Birthday Wishes," "A Prayer When a Child Is Born," "A Letter to Newlyweds," and other excerpts from *Best Wishes* by Harold E. Kohn. Copyright © 1969, published by Wm. B. Eerdmans Publishing Co.

ALEC J. LANGFORD for an excerpt from his writings.

IVA LILLGE for "Planting Time." Copyright © 1980 by Iva Lillge.

I. J. LUNDGREN for "A Teenage Son."

BASILLA E. NEILAN for an excerpt from her writings. All rights reserved.

ROY PEARSON for an excerpt from his writings.

MAY RICHSTONE for an excerpt from her writings.

HAROLD A. SCHULZ for "These Days."

LOUISE H. SCLOVE for "House Blessing" from *Death and General Putnam and 101 Other Poems* by Arthur Guiterman. Copyright 1935 by E. P. Dutton, Co., Inc.

MYRA SCOVEL for "Every Boy Should Have a Dog" and another excerpt from her writings.

RALPH W. SEAGER for "Daughter," "He Was My Teacher," "Familiar Stranger," "5th of July Parade," and "Grandfather's Cane."

W. HEWLETT STITH for "On Anniversaries and Birthdays" from the *Virginia Advocate*, March 20, 1980.

TIMKEN SENIOR HIGH SCHOOL for "The Student Creed."

ELTON TRUEBLOOD for selected excerpts from his writings.

MRS. LOUIS UNTERMEYER for "Prayer for a New House" from the writings of Louis Untermeyer.

JOHN UPDIKE for an excerpt from his writings.

JUNE WEAVER for "Family Portrait."

HOWARD C. WILKINSON for "Commencement Prayer."

ESTATE OF LIN YUTANG for an excerpt from the writings of Lin Yutang.

In addition to the authors and representatives listed below, acknowledgment is also made to the *P.E.O. Record* in which the following selections appeared:

NAOMI HOLT BARNARD for "Remember?"

VIRGINIA COVEY BOSWELL for "The Keepsakes Of Christmas," "To a Daughter Graduating," "Rocker Full of Love" which also appeared in *Home Life*, Sept. 1973, and "The Kitchen Door" which also appeared in *Ideals* magazine.

BETTY HUMBLES BROWN for "A Mother's Morning Prayer."

DOROTHY L. CAMPBELL for "Old Clock."

BONNIE DARSIE for "The Angel with the Band Aid," written during a morning service of Union Church of Manila.

BEVERLY WITHAM EDELBLUTE for "Christmas Pageant."

JEAN EVANS for "Chrismas Bread."

VIRGINIA S. GABLE for "Occupation: Mother."

MAY GRAY for "Bells, Starlight And Song."

VIRGINIA SHEARER HOPPER for "To My Daughter."

VIVIAN C. ISGRIG for "To a Granddaughter."

JANET DOUGLAS MANCHESTER for "The Children's Christmas Dreams." All rights reserved.

VIRGINIA McEWAN for "Let Us Love Abundantly."

RUTH NEAL for "Which."

MARGARET RORKE for "Love" from *An Old Cracked Cup* by Margaret Rorke. Copyright © 1980 by Northwood Institute Press.

RUTH STAUNTON for "Oremus."

EUNICE L. SWALLUM for "Rendezvous."

CHARLOTTE A. SWEDE for "Full Measure."

PEGGY URSTAD for "The Joy of Children."

GLADYS D. WHITNEY for "Miracle."

233

Acknowledgment is also made to the following authors:

Grace A. Auringer, Kay Andrew, Edith Kent Battle, Alan Beck, George Benson, Christian Nestell Bovee, Hal Boyle, Brother Lawrence, Myrtle G. Burger, Barbara Burrow, Richard C. Cabot, Anne Campbell, Amy Carmichael, Nan Carroll, Joyce Cary, William Douglas Chamberlain, Helen P. Chapman, Catherine C. Coblentz, Jan Compton, Josephine Rice Creelman, Lois Mae Cuhel, Rose Darrough, Sir Humphrey Davy, Louis De Louk, Agnes De Mille, Thomas Dreier, Henry Drummond, Ouida Smith Dunnam, Albert Einstein, Charles W. Eliot, Richard L. Evans, Merritt W. Faulkner, Henry Gregor Felsen, John Ferguson, R. K. Fletcher, Jessie Merle Franklin, Buckminster Fuller, Ruch Gagliardo, John Garrett, Winfred Ernest Garrison, Louis E. Gelineau, Harry Golden, Almeta Hilty Good, Abbie Graham, Louise Hajek, Hattie Vose Hall, James Hamilton, Hildegarde Hawthorne, Agnes MacCarthy Hickey, Leslie Pinckney Hill, Nellie Womack Hines, Lord Houghton, Lavetta Hummel, Aldous Huxley, L. P. Jacks, Florence Pedigo Jansson, Charles Jefferys, Barbara A. Jones, Thomas S. Jones, Jr., W. C. Jones, John Henry Jowett, Helen Keller, James Keller, Lilian Leveridge, Lawrence O. Lineberger, Richard Livingstone, Wilson MacDonald, Justice W. McEachren, Clyde McGee, Gabriela Mistral, Roselle Mercier Montgomery, Robert J. Mueller, Klara Munkres, Catherine Parmenter Newell, Ann Osborne, Everett W. Palmer, Katherine Parker, Paul Calvin Payne, Wilfred A. Peterson, Jean Fuller Rausch, Henry Rische, Ernestine Schuman-Heink, Ruth Smeltzer, Ralph W. Sockman, Lena Sorabji, Adlai Stevenson, Hester Suthers, Booth Tarkington, Helen Taylor, Jeremy Taylor, Gilbert Thomas, Thomas Tiplady, Charles Hanson Towne, Ester May Walker, Harold Blake Walker, Alma L. Weixelbaum, Edward Whiting, B. Y. Williams, Kay Wissinger, Gertrude Dower Wolohon, and Leland Foster Wood.

INDEX OF CONTRIBUTORS

INDEX OF TITLES AND FIRST LINES

Prose selection titles are in italic type; poetry selection titles
are in quotation marks; first lines have no punctuation.

239